contemporary Korean poetry

contemporary Korean poetry

translated and edited by Kim Jaihiun

Mosaic Press
Oakville-Buffalo-London

CANADIAN CATALOGUING IN PUBLICATION DATA

Contemporary Korean Poetry
ISBN 0-88962-561-1

1. Korean poetry - 20th century - Translations into English. I. Kim,
Jaihiun Joyce, 1934-

PL984.E3K5 1994   895.7'1408   C94-931146-4

Published by MOSAIC PRESS, P.O. Box 1032 Oakville, Ontario, L6J 5E9,
Canada. Offices and warehouse at 1252 Speers Road, Units #1 & 2, Oakville,
Ontario, L6L 5N9, Canada.

**Published with the generous support of the Korean Culture and Arts
Foundation.**

Mosaic Press acknowledges the assistance of the Canada Council and the
Ontario Arts Council in support of its publishing programme.

Copyright © 1994, Jaihiun Kim
Design by Susan Parker
Typeset by Heather Wade

Printed and Bound in Canada
ISBN 0-88962-561-1 PB

MOSAIC PRESS:
In Canada:
    MOSAIC PRESS, 1252 Speers Rd, Units 1 & 2, Oakville, Ontario,
L6L 5N9, Canada. P.O. Box 1032, Oakville, Ontario L6J 5E9
In the United States:
    Mosaic Press, 85 River Rock Drive, Suite 202, Buffalo, N.Y., 14207
In the U.K.:
    John Calder (Publishers) Ltd., 9-15 Neal Street, London, WCZH 9TU,
England

TABLE OF CONTENTS

NOTE ON THE TRANSLATOR

Poet and translator born in 1934 in Korea, Jaihiun J. Kim was educated both in Seoul at Hankuk University of Foreign Studies and in the United States at the University of Massachusetts, where he earned an M.A. and M.F.A. degrees. The World University honored him with a doctorate in literature. Currently professor of English at Ajou University, he has taught English and creative writing in an American university before returning home to Korea. Highly praised as a talented poet writing in English as well as in his native tongue, Kim has translated approximately 2300 Korean poems into English, including Chinese poems, in addition to 10 volumes of his own poems, four of them in Korean: *Revolt of Soil* (1975), *Drifting Life* (1979), *Singing Weeds* (1982), *A Certain Hug* (1986), and *Rainbow in the City* (1991); the others in English: *Detour* (1982), *A Pigsty Happiness* (1973) both published in the U.S., *Home-thought* (1976), *Dawning* (1976), *Reed-plumes* (1979) and *Nature Man* (1988). His poems in English have been published mostly in the U.S. in *Kauri, Overflow, Kayak, United Poet, American Poet, and Prairie Poet.* His translations of English from the Korean include *Azaleas* by Sowol Kim (1973), *The Immortal Voice* (1974), *Twenty-three Poems of Yun Sook Moh* (1975), *Master Poems from Modern Korea* (1980), *The Contemporary Korean Poets* (1980), *Master Sijo Poems from Korea* (1982), *The Silence of Love* (1985), *O Mother and Sisters* (1985), a collection of verses for children, *A Sijo Selection* (1986), in collaboration with others, *Classical Korean Poetry* (1986), *Korean Poetry Today* (1987), in collaboration with others, *Classical Korean Poetry* (1986), *Korean Poetry Today* (1987), *Poems by Zen Masters* (1988), *Cold Mountain* (1989) and *Traditional Korean Verse* (1991), an anthology of modern sijo poems. His English-to-Korean translations include *Selected Poems of Emily Dickinson* (1976), *Invisible Man* (1987) by R. Ellison, *Selected Poems of Irving Layton* (1986), *The Fixer* (1987) by M. Malamud, *Selected Poems of William Wordsworth* (1991). His collection of essays *Lovers and Thinkers* came out in 1991. Now Kim is working on another collection of his poems in English, in addition to a series of Korean poetry for a foreign publisher.

PREFACE

I have prepared this anthology with the aim of providing the reader with a bird's-eye view of modern Korean poetry, with its best sampling, from the 1920s to the early 1980s, best in the sense that it best represents the varied aspects of Korean poetry. The limited number of poems in this collection can hardly claim to be the best of the whole bulk of Korean poetry. One master poet's work may excel scores of poems by as many poets, although the best in quality can often be relative or vary from taste to taste, from criterion to criterion. Therefore, I have tried to take as objective a view as possible in my selection, to live up to the popular concept of culling the choicest of the choice, except for some works whose use for translation has not been allowed for one reason or another. And, again, in the process of selection, I have been obliged to exclude a number of poems which fall, I feel, within the category of the untranslatable.

As is the case with many other anthologists, I have found it necessary to set a limit on the time-span. Naturally, this by no means leaves out recent works of those who won recognition as poets in the early years. It is my belief that a historical evaluation of the achievement of the poets who have emerged since the mid-1980s will have to wait for the perspective of time. And in order not to turn too much attention to a few poets at the expense of many others, I have limited the number of individual representations.

I have arranged the poets roughly in chronological order for convenience, though poets may have preceded others in establishing their literary names. In a sense, the whole gamut of eight decades of modern Korean poetry may well fit in the period of a modern Korea as seen at this point in time. On the whole, with the exception of a handful of poems unavailable for inclusion, the poets represented here can be regarded as major figures standing for the significant trends in shaping modern Korean poetry.

June 1992
Seoul, Korea   J.K.

INTRODUCTION

The earliest Korean poetry was written as far back as the rise of Korean civilization. "Song for Holden Orioles," the earliest extant poem, composed in Chinese characters by King Yuri (ca. 19 B.C. - 17 A.D.) of the Koguryo Kingdom (ca. 3 B.C. - 668 A.D.), reads as follows:

> Golden orioles are flitting about,
> Male and female enjoying each other.
> Left alone to myself in solitude,
> Who shall I return home with?*

It is obvious that volumes of poems were produced during the fourteen centuries until the end of the Koryo dynasty (918-1392). To our great regret, however, we have left to us only 25 poems which have survived the ravages of time. *Hyang'ga*, native songs as they were called, are the poetic heritage of the Shilla Kingdom. Most of them are thematically related to Buddhism. For instance, a widow prays for the bliss of her husband's departed soul in "Song for Nirvana":

> O moon, are you proceeding
> as far as the Western Land?
> Please go and tell Buddha
> Of Immeasurable Bliss
> that there's one poor soul left behind
> praying, her hands joined,
> before Merciful Amitabha
> that her husband may enter Nirvana.
> For herself, she only desires
> to have forty wishes come true.

The *hyang'ga*, four to ten lines in length, evolved into the *tan'ga* or the short songs, typically of three lines, in the latter part of the Koryo Dynasty. *Sijo*, an appellation given to *tan'ga* in the 18th century, settled into a fixed form as late as the mid-15th century with the

---

* A story is told of the composition of the poem. King Yuri on his return home from hunting found that the more favored of his two wives had left him after a quarrel with the other. He hastened after her and pleaded with her in vain to come back. On his way back he chanced to see a couple of orioles flying about in a tree.

invention and propagation of the Korean alphabet, *han 'gul*. Surviving *sijo* poems including those written throughout the whole period of the Chosun Dynasty (1392-1910), approximate 3,600 in number. While the tradition of *sijo* poetry has persisted down to the present, old Korea was brought to an abrupt end in 1910 with the onset of the Japanese colonization of Korea, which lasted until the end of the Second World War in 1945.

Naturally the history of modern Korean poetry is short for no substantial body of poems with modern sensibility and outlook appeared before the early part of the 20th century, when Korea started to awake from her long sleep of hermitage. Whereas traditional literature was primarily nurtured under the influence of Chinese literature, modern literature began to take shape with the impact of Western literary thought at the turn of the century. In other words, the early embryonic drive started with Practical Learning (1170s-1820s) by bringing Korea into direct contact with the West, ushering in the Era of Enlightenment, which extended roughly from 1880 to 1910.

Impelled by the surges of reform in political, educational, and social systems during the period, Korean literature was ready to embark on its modernization under the banner of New Style Literature, borne by Namson Ch'oe in poetry and Kwangsu Yi in fiction. Ch'oe's "*To the Boy from the Sea*" came out in 1908 in his own magazine **Sonyon** (The Boy) and Yi's early works in 1917. It must be pointed out in this context that, though these two figures are often mentioned as the fathers of modern Korean literature, they acted more as catalysts of modernizing Korean literature as a whole. More concerned with the didactic function of literature, they tended to employ art as a means of enlightening the people and enhancing social progress. To be more precise, Korean poetry started, in the historical perspective, with Yohan Chu and Ok Kim. Korean literature in general and Korean poetry in particular did not break out of its own shell of didacticism before the late 1910s, when the currents of 19th century European literary thoughts flowed into the literary world of Korea almost a century late.

Swayed neither by the influence of the sermonization of new style poems nor by the outburst of emotion of diluted romanticism, Chu and Kim succeeded in setting up a landmark with t heir lyrics written in the tradition of folk balladry. That is, it was with Chu and Kim that modern Korean poetry began to individualize itself. It seems advisable to note in passing that romanticism in Korea was not an exact copy of the western pattern. As in other areas of art, a comparison of Korean literature ought to be made in the context of Korean culture. It is true that poets looked into themselves to probe their own lives for sensation, like their counterparts in European countries, but the romantic notion of the unity of man and nature added an embittered spice of sorrow and melancholy to the spirit of the times. Then, toward the mid-1920s Chu and Kim were succeeded in turn by Tonghwan Kim and Sowol Kim. Unmistakably the best poet of the period, Sowol Kim by far overshadowed Ok Kim, his teacher and mentor, and distinguished himself by crystallizing the vernacular sentiments and pathos of the people in a string of gem-like poems such as "*The Azaleas*", "*Flowers in the Mountains*", and "*Invocation*", to name a few. He was the first to have a wide range of interests and a deep knowledge of nature. He saw nature not merely as a center of beauty but also as a source of intimations of life. By subtle manipulation of paradox he made things in nature vehicles for the expression of human situations. Contemporary with him, Tonghwan Kim, like Yongno Pyon and Tongmyong Kim, reminisced on the beauty of the lost land. "When the River Breaks Loose" and "Snow Is Falling" are noteworthy pieces of the period. And his "Frontier Night", though suffering from structural laxness, is the first attempt made at a memorable epic poem. Nevertheless, the majority of the lyric pieces written about this period are limited in scale and range, and mainly concerned with sentiment. In the late 1920s Sanghwa Yi and Yong'un Han gave muscle to Korean poetry by incorporating into it the texture of metaphysical depth and insight into human consciousness. Despite his plunge into a romantic cave of sensuality and melancholy, Yi was able to give articulate shape to his experience:

Madonna, soon the day dawns, come over quickly
before a temple bell mocks us.
Let us go, your hands clinging around my neck,
to the everlasting land in company with this night. (from "To My Bedroom)

Himself a devoted Buddhist monk as well as a patriot, Yong'un Han immortalized himself by turning out a series of poems. His tour de force was evident in his collected poems *The Silence of Love* (1925), which embodies the metaphysical complexity and paradox of the human condition through Buddhistic formulas as well as poetic expression. According to Buddhism, the self and the object are transmutable from the ontological view point, as long as *karma* exists between the two, and with the loss of the *karma* relationship, the self and the object perish at the same time. The focal idea is illustrated in "*I Do Not Know*":

Burnt-out ashes turn to fuel again.
Whose lamp is my heart that burns
Flickering all night long?

When we think of history, we tend to think of a time-span characterized by certain events of consequence. It was in 1910 that Korea, after nearly a decade of the loss of her independent movement suffered defeat before the brutalities of the oppressors. The awakening national consciousness gathered momentum but the overwhelming sense of loss and despair soon plunged the nation again into darkness. In the midst of gloom, the prevailing sense of defeatism gave way to frustration and pessimism. Amid the vortex of decadence and confusion emerged a band of communist-oriented poets, who considered art merely as a means with which to fight the oppressors. Their works, however, hardly met the aesthetic standard of art. Way off from the chaos of the period, Sanghwa Y found the articulate voices of the time in his, "*Does Spring Come to These Forfeited Fields?*":

> Does spring come to this land no more our own,
> to these forfeited fields?
> Bathed in the sun I go as in a dream along a lane
> that cuts across paddy-fields like parted hair
> to where the blue sky and the green fields merge.

Toward the early 1930s the excessive heart-thumping and morbid sentimentalism ebbed away with the advent of intellectualism. At the same time the raving clamor of communist themes was on its way in favor of art for art's sake. Yongnag Kim, Chiyong Chong and Sokchong Shin were among the finest poets of the period. Yongchol Park excelled more in theorizing about writing than in actual composition. Remember for "*The Departing Boat*", Park enjoys a reputation more as a fine critic than a fine poet. Seriously concerned with the form and musicality of language, Yongnag Kim successfully created a dream-like atmosphere through the harmony of sense and sound. Chiyong Chong, on the other hand, carved image-reliefs in the modernistic tradition of the West. Sokchong Shin, well remembered as the pastoral poet, spent the greater part of his boyhood in the remote countryside, where he developed into a conscientious craftsman, with a wide range of human interest and an intimate knowledge of country life. About this period, Kirim Kim made his appearance. Turning his back on the lyric tradition of poetry, he refused to follow his predecessors by seeking pure aesthetic ideals. Parnassian at heart, he introduced into Korean poetry a gallery of imagery devoid of the sentimental and the maudlin. His "*Weatherchart*", in more than four hundred lines, reads in part:

> The channel of the sea
> wriggles alive
> like the snake back

where scales
bristle up;
young mountain-ranges
draped in colorful Arabian costumes;
wind smoothly skirts
the shore like Saracen's silk.

Kirim Kim was the first to acquaint the reader with western poets like
T.E. Hulme, Ezra Pound, W.H. Auden and T.S. Eliot. Kwangkyun
Kim, who followed his example, wrote poems many of which surpassed
Kirim Kim's. Written in the modernistic tradition, his "*The Lyricism
of an Autumn Day*" and "*Snowy Night*" were considered the best pieces
of the period. About this time Sang Yi made his debut as a new poet.
He showed disgust with the prevailing modes of expression and the
conformist spirit of man by experimenting with surrealistic technique
and employing Joycean stream-of-consciousness in his works. His
"*Flower-tree*", for instance, can hardly make sense if handled on the
surface level of consciousness:

In the midst of wilderness there stands a flower tree,
with no other tree near it. It blossoms in earnest as much
as it yearns in earnest for its companion somewhere.
And yet it cannot get to its fellow tree it is so much
in love with. I run away toward another tree as if I were
the very flower tree.

In the late 1930s poetry and literary magazines cropped up like
the mushrooms after a rain. To this galaxy of poets belonged Ch'on-
myong No, Kwangsop Kim, Chongju So, Sokcho Shin and Ch'iwan Yu.
In revolt against the lifelessness and sand-dryness of modernist poems.
So, for one, breathed vitality into Korean poetry. He sought for the life
force through his magic wand of manipulating language, achieving some
of the best pieces such as "*The Snake*" and "*Midday*". He gave through
the mastery of his work the direction Korean poetry had to take. Yu was
interested in seeking the essence of life and the identity of his own being.
Sangyong Kim, by contrast, felt happy on his retirement to the countryside.
Other poets of this generation were Ch'ongmyong No and Yunsuk Mo.
Perhaps in the long tradition of the regret and pain couched in poems by
women, No's work concerned grief and bitterness of thwarted hope while
Mo's projected a bright outlook of life. The 1930s witnessed before the
close of the decade the three members of the **Blue Deer Group**, which
links up with the lyric tradition of Korean poetry. Tujin Park, for instance,

sought in nature the meaning of man's existence. Mogwol Park waved his magic rod over language to fashion rare gems, mostly in short poems. Lastly, Chihun Cho resorted to things past in recreating the beauty of the country. Again at this period Chongju So, now diverted from the Dyonysiac life-fever, egan to turn to pure lyricism in his "*Beside The Chrysanthemum*" and "*The Nightingale Path*". Ch'ihwan Yu sustained touch with the hard realities of the nation.

Thanks to the general panic during the war years, the 1950s saw few significant literary activities until well after the war ended. A rare exception was made in the case of the two poets. Tongju Yun and Yuksa Yi, both of whose poems were published after the war. Yi's "*Vortex*" gave us a graphic picture of the dark times that tormented the nation:

> Gashed by the slashing of a harsh season
> I was driven at last to the north,
> Where the bored heaven succumbed to the height
> and black frost cut my flesh.
> I do not know where to stretch my leg;
> where to land a single step.

In his "*Wilderness*" Yi found salvation only through his own sacrifice made for the good of his fellowmen. The image of self-sacrifice is remarkably carved in "*The Cross*" by Tongju Yun:

> Should I have been allowed the cross
> as was Jesus Christ
> Who suffered but was happy,
> I would gladly hang my own head
> and let my blood flow in quiet
> like a flower that blooms
> under the darkening skies.

At last *"The Day"* came that Hun Shim desperately and prophetically had wished for:

> When the day comes at last
> Mt. Samgak will leap in a joyful dance.
> When the day comes the waters of the Han
> will toss and roll in delight.
> If only the day comes before my life closes
> I will go and beat my head against the town bell
> to ring to the crows winging across the night sky;

Even if my skull were crushed to pieces
I would gladly die
and I shall have no regrets.

The liberation period after the war saw a group of poets, among
whom were Suyong Kim, Inhwan Park, Pyonghwa Cho, Tongjip Shin,
Sang Ku, Hyonggi Yi and Tongju Yi. Most prolific of all, Cho
vignetted the arabesque of city life and the loneliness of man. Suyong
Kim emphasized the commitment of art to society, his work laced with
suggestiveness and puns. Tongju Yi wove the tapestry of native
Korean sentiment with the music of language.

The Korean war (1950-1953) virtually made a turning point in
contemporary Korean poetry, within the framework of its long and
diverse tradition. By and large, we can look at the post-war picture in
three different frameworks. One is persistent in keeping to the agelong
tradition. Among those who fit into this framework are Chaesam Park and
Tongju Yi. Another group of poets has made a successful attempt at
creating a new tradition with a strong dash of experimentalism as well
exemplified in "*The Poppy*" by Songyong Park:

Ready to faint when held;
to crumble when hugged,
that flower is no other than the opium
poppy whose fume once drowsed
the whole of China.
Just a frail annual plant,
it flares up my sunset garden
with its charm and beauty.

Hijin Park adds to the vitality of the group. The third group likes
to be identified with Suyong Kim, who defined the function of artists
as serving the betterment of human conditions, in a sense different from
what the earlier propagandists pretended to claim. To this group
belonged Tongyop Shin and Kyongnim Shin. Contemporary with them
are a number of young poets like Tonggyu Hwang, Yongtae Kim, and
Huran Kim, who distinguished themselves during the 1960s. From the
late 1960s to the mid-1970s quite a few new poets made their voices
heard. With varied experiences and sensibilities, the new faces include
Yojong Kim, Yangshik Kim, Un'gyo Kang, and Chaehyon Kim
(Jaihiun Kim) who received intensive training in creative writing in the
United States before returning home to Korea to publish his poems in
his native tongue. The three younger poets Sugwon Song, Hyongman
Ho and Chonggwon Cho are on their own as distinctive voices. Lastly,
highlighting his dogged resistance and protest against the establishment

and his craving for the national reunification, Namju Kim represents many voices in the 1980s following in the wake of Chiha Kim, Pong'u Park and Tongjip Shin before him.

Finally, I should like to thank all those poets who have allowed me to translate their works. Thanks are due to Larchwood Publication Ltd. for giving me permission to use the "Introduction" in this anthology. Thanks are also due to the Korean Culture and Arts Foundation whose generosity has made this anthology possible, apart from the willingness on the part of Mosaic Press. I appreciate my colleague Mr. Hurcherson at Ajou University and Mr. Jack Large at Wonkwang University who kindly proofread my manuscript.

INDEX OF TITLES

E

F

G

H

I

L

M

N

O

P

R

S

HAN, Yong-un (1879-1944). A native of Hongsong, South Ch'ungchong province, a devoted Buddhist monk since his early years, Han was one of the 33 members who in 1919 signed the historical document to declare Korea independent of the Japanese colonial control. His poems concern his philosophical meditation on nature and the mystery of human existence. His books are *The Silence of Love* (1926) and *The Complete Works* (1973).

The Silence of Love

Love is gone, gone is my love.
Tearing himself away from me he has gone
on a little path that stretches in the splendor
of a green hill into the autumn-tinted woods.
Our last oath, shining and enduring
like a gold-mosaicked flower,
has turned to cold ashes, blown away in the breath of wind.
I remember his poignant first kiss and its memory has wrought
a complete change in my destiny,
then withdrawn into oblivion.
I hear not his sweet voice; I see not his fair looks.
Since it is human to love, I, alert, dreaded
a parting to come when we met.
The separation came so suddenly
it broke my heart with renewed sorrow.
Yet, I know parting can only destroy our love
if it causes futile tears to fall.
I would rather transfer the surge of this sorrow
onto the summit of hopefulness.
As we dread parting when we meet, so,
we promise to meet again when we part.
Though my love is gone, I am not parted from love;
an untiring love-song envelops the silence of love.

I Do not Know

Whose step is the paulownia leaf that falls silently
in vertical wavelets against the windless sky?
Whose looks are those patches of blue that peep
through the cracks of the dark dreadful clouds,
driven by the west wind after a long spell of rain?
Whose breath is this subtle scent that permeates the air
wafting through the green moss on an ancient tree,
no flower near, to lure the quiet sky above an ancient pagoda?
Whose song is the little stream that flows,
God know from where, purling over the pebbles?
Whose ode is the evening glow that graces the dying day
as it steps, lotus-flower soft, on the infinite seas
and touches the edgeless sky with its delicate hands?
The burnt-out ashes turn to earth again.
Whose lamp is my heart that burns all night long,
I know not for whom?

The Ferryboat and the Traveler

I am a ferryboat. A traveler, you trample me down
with muddy shoes. I take you aboard to cross
the river. With you held in my arms, I go across
the currents, deep, shallow, or rapid.
If you do not turn up, I await you from dawn
to dusk, despite the wind, rain, or snow.
Yet, once you've crossed the river, you do not look back on me.
But I believe you will be coming back some day.
I grow old and worn-out waiting for you
day after day,
I am a ferryboat. You are a traveler.

PYON, Yongno (1898-1961). Born in Seoul and educated at San Jose College, U.S.A., Pyon taught at Ehwa Women's University. In the initial stage of modern Korean poetry, Pyon made himself conspicuous by his use of modernistic technique dashed with lyricism. His books are *The Mind of Korea* (1924), and *Azales* (1947) written in English.

Non-gae*

Her holy anger was
deeper than faith;
her burning passion was
stronger than love.

On the waves
bluer than kidney beans in bloom
her heart flows in ripples
redder than red poppies.

Her charming eyebrows
poised aloft in grace;
her pomegranate lips
kissed death.

On the waves
bluer than kidney beans in bloom
her heart flows in ripples
redder than red poppies.

The rippling waves
will flow forever blue;
her fair soul
will be blazing forever red.

On the waves
bluer than kidney beans in bloom
her heart flows in ripples
redder than red poppies.

* A legendary courtesan, patriotism incarnate. She was invited to the victory
celebration of a group of Japanese generals who had led their invading armies into
Korea in the 16th century. When the party reached its height she embraced one of the
generals to throw herself with him off a cliff into the river.

Spring Rain

A voice is calling, low and quiet;
I go out,yes, I go out to see
A drowsy milky cloud drift
As if in a hurry yet leisurely enough,
across the azure sky.
How I miss something I've not lost!

A voice is calling, low and quiet;
I go out, yes, go out to feel
A breath of flowers fade,
Trembling and invisible,
In the dim memories of the past
and luxuriates in its own scent.

A voice is calling, low and quiet;
I go out, yes, go out to see
No trace of milky cloud nor flower-breath
But silver threads of spring rain
Falling quietly like a brooding thought,
Fit to wet a pigeon's pink feet.
How I expect someone who will not come!

CHU, Yohan (1900-1979). Born in Pyongyang, North Korea, Chu was educated both in Tokyo and Shanghai. A pioneer of modern Korean poetry, he first demonstrated modernity in poetry by his own poems being published in **Ch'anjo** (Creation), a literary magazine given to introducing romanticism in Korea. His books are *Beautiful Dawn* (1924), *Peach Blossoms* (1930) and *Poems of Three Poets*, in collaboration with two other poets.

The Sound of Rain

Rain is falling.
Night quietly unfolds her wings.
Rain talks in whispers like chickens
in the yard peeping among themselves.

The moon has gone thread-thin;
Warm breezes start to rise as if
The spring trickles down from the stars.
Rain is falling this dark night.

Rain is falling
Gently like a friendly guest calling.
I open the window to greet him.
Rain is falling, quiet and invisible.

In the yard, outside the window
and on the roof rain is falling.
Rain is falling to bring pleasant tidings
for my private joy.

Fireworks

The day wanes. The evening-glow sinks into the lonely river, crimsoning the western sky. With sunset comes another night when I must cry my heart out in the shade of an apricot tree. Today is Buddha's birthday, the eighth of the fourth month, and crowds of people throng about in the streets, all soaked in a festive mood. But why should I be left alone in sorrow amidst the stir and bustle of the celebration?
Ever so many balls of fire are dancing madly. As I watch them from the gate of city wall, the smell of water and sandy flats assails my nostrils, fulgent torches swaying and scraping the sky. And then unsatisfied, they go on consuming themselves. A youth, with darkness cutting into his heart, tries to toss his purple dreams of the past into the waters of the river. Can the heartless flow of the river

stop his thin shadow? How can flowers stay fresh when plucked off? As good as dead in life, lost in the thought of my beloved, shall I let this flame burn out my heart, burn down my sorrow? Only yesterday I dragged my lead-heavy feet to the graveyards and found flower-buds unfolding from where they had been lying dead in the winter. But how about love's springtime? Will it never come back? I would rather put an end to it all, plunging into the water. Yet, who will ever pity me, lament over my loss? Suddenly *crack, crack,* shoots up a rocket fire, a shower of sparks spread fanwise. I come to. The explosive laughter of the spectators sounds as if to mock and accuse me. Would that I lived a more passionate life, a flaming life, like those fireworks that leap up their tongues from smouldering smoke, even in their burning agony. My burning heart craves for something to match it.

When the warm April breeze strokes across the river, the crowds in white start to mill about on Peony Hill* by the clear river. And at the touch of wind, the fiery wavelets laugh a lunatic laugh and the fish dart, scared, into the sand-bed for shelter. Aboard the boat sliding down the currents, figures of men rock to the sleepy dancing rhythms, shadows flickering in a peal of laughter, and then a youthful courtesan chants in a drawn-out voice under a lantern hanging overhead. Now the blazing fireworks subside, glass after glass of wine wears me out. I lie stretched on the filthy bottom of the boat, idle tears bathing my cheeks. Sick of the incessant dinning of the drum, some dash out of the boat, their eyes flashing with refuelled desire, the candlelight guttering drowsily on the rumpled skirt-folds. And the oarlocks alone squeak as if to give some meaning; they weight down my heart.

Look how the river laughs! A weird laugh. The chill waters laugh looking up to the blackening sky. The boat comes into view, gliding down the waves, oarlocks squeaking, accompanied by sorrow in every gust of wind. Row the boat against the rapid currents of the Taedong River* all the way down to the Nungna Isle*, where your sweetheart awaits standing barefoot on the bank. Head straight where she is. What of the chill gust rising in the wake of the boat? What of the weird laughter? What of the dark and depressed heart of a love-lorn youth? Light follows shadow. Seize the day. That is the only certitude. Boys, live today, enjoy tonight, delight in your own red-flaming torch, your red-lips, your eyes and your red tears.

* Place names and a river name in North Korea.

YI, Sanghwa (1900-1941). Born in Taegu, North Kyongsang province, Yi studied French at Tokyo University of Foreign Studies, Japan. Limited in number, his poems represent the romantic trend of the twenties. He succeeded in crystallizing the misery of the oppressed nation into "*Does Spring Come to These Forfeited Fields?*" His poems, sixteen in all, are contained in Sanghwa and Sowol (1951).

Does Spring Come to These Forfeited Fields?

Does spring come to the land no more our own,*
to these forfeited fields?
Bathed in the sun I go as if in a dream along a lane
that cuts across paddy-fields like parted hair
to where the blue sky and the green fields merge.
You mute heaven and silent fields,
I do not feel I have come here on my own;
tell me if I am driven by you or some hidden force.
The breeze murmurs in my ears and
strokes my garment at every step;
the larks behind the clouds are trilling
in joy like maidens across the hedge.
You rich green fields of corn,
I see you have washed your tresses
in the gentle rain that fell last night.
I feel so refreshed and light in t he head.
Alone as I am, my steps are cheerful,
for the kind water in the ditch
rushes in a waltz past the thirsty fields.
with sweet songs of lullaby.
Swallows and butterflies, be gentle and modest.
I must say hello to the cockscomb-blossoming village.
I wish to have another look at those fields
weeded by women, their hair oil-shining.

Hand me a hoe so that I may work
in an honest sweat; that I may walk on this soil
soft as full breasts till my ankles grow numb with pain.
My soul years for something infinite as
that of children frolicking on the riverbank.
Tell me what it is you are craving for, where you
are headed. I am impatient to know.
Soaked in the smell of the greening earth

I walk all day long limping between the green of sorrow
and joy as if possessed by the spirit of spring.
But now that the land is no more our own
spring can no longer be our own.

* indicative of the Japanese colonial rule.

CHONG, Chiyong (1901-195?). Born in Okchon, North Ch'ungchong province, Chong studied English literature at Tojisha University, Japan. During World War II he taught at high schools and after the war was Professor of English at Ehwa Women's University. He was forced into North Korea during the Korean War (1950-1953). One of the most influential poets during the twenties, Chong brought vigor and modernistic images dashed with vernacular sentiments into Korean poetry. His books are **Collected Poems** (1935), **Paeknok Tarn** (1941) and **Selected Poems** (1946).

Native Village

When I come back home, to my native village
I find it not as sweet as it used to be.

The pheasants brood as before in the mountains
and cuckoos sing their seasonal carols.

But my heart is homeless, belonging nowhere
and drifts as a cloud over a far-away port.

Again today as I alone go up a hilltop
a flower smiles sweetly, my lips gone dry and bitter.

When I come back home, to my native village
the blue expanse of sky spreads high and endless.

The Summit

Cliffs are tinged red
as with cinnabar.
The waters flow dew-clear.
Poised on a perilous perch of a tree
a red-winged bird pecks at fruit.
Wild grape-vines have budded green.
A scented snake lies coiled up in plateau-dreams.
The summit of height towers, majestic like death,
where birds of passage first visit;
the crescent moon sinks
and a double rainbow begins to form.
A view from below makes it look as high as Orion.
I step onto the topmost crag
a white flower the size of a star wavers.
I brace my feet, my legs dandelion-stalk thin.
The east sea where the sun rises
seems to beat against my cheeks
like a flap flapping in the breeze.

Nostalgic Urge

Winding eastward through a wide plain
the brook murmured an old tale on its way;
a brindle ox lowed lazily
in the golden glow of sunset.
How can I ever forget that place even in dreams?

When fire was going out in an earthen brazier,
the wind galloped across the desert plain;
resting his head on a straw-roll
my old father would take a nap.
How can I ever forget that place even in dreams?

Brought up with soil, my heart was aglow
with longing for the bright blue sky;
Once I shot an arrow at random into the air
and got soaked while searching the wet bushes.
How can I ever forget that place even in dreams?

My sister would wear her raven hair long
like night waves in a legendary sea:
my simple-hearted wife led a plain life,
dispensing with foot-wear for all seasons.
They would often glean a field with the sun on their backs.
How can I ever forget that place even in dreams?

Under the skies studded sparsely with stars,
I would go for a secret sand-castle;
autumn crows cawed winging over a thatched hut
where I would join my friends and chat around a dim-lit lamp.
How can I ever forget that place even in dreams?

KIM, Tonghwan (1901-19??). Born in Kyongsong, North Hamgyong province, North Korea, Kim went to Tokyo University, Japan. He was taken by force to North Korea during the Korean war (1950-1953). He started his literary career with *The Frontier Night* regarded as the first epic poem ever written in modern Korea. His poems embrace nationalistic ideals in simple and rhythmic cadences and *A Wing Returned* (1962), published by his family.

When the River Breaks Loose

When the river breaks loose
A boat will come;
Aboard her will come
My sweet love.

If my love comes not
her word will come aboard the boat.
I wait by the riverside today
And return home, empty-hearted.

If my love comes
This grief in me will melt away
As a river stark-frozen in midwinter
Breaks loose sooner or later.

The river will break loose in no time.
What keeps it from melting, I wonder?
I wait by the riverside today
And return home, empty-hearted.

The Boatsong of the Sungari

Clouds scud in patches on the dawning sky.
Yo-heave-ho, yo-heave-ho, let us move on.
Where clouds sail
Sails my heart too.

We've left our country a thousand *li** behind.
Yo-heave-ho, yo-heave-ho, let us move on.
We've come a thousand *li* so far;
We have a thousand *li* to go yet.
We've left our country
With love tied to it.

Yo-heave-ho, yo-heave-ho, let us move on.
Even the waters of the Sungari moan.
Yo-heave-ho, yo-heave-ho, let us move one.
Is the river weeping alone?
We are weeping too.

*16 *li* equals a mile.

KIM, Tongmyong (1901-1966). Born in Kangnung, Kangwon province, Kim studied theology at Aoyama Academy, Japan. His career ranged widely as a teacher, newspaper editorial writer and a National Assembly man. Under the Japanese colonial rule he left the city for the countryside where he wrote with a nostalgic urge for his country before it had been overrun with the oppressors. His works include *My Lyre* (1930), *The Banana Plant* (19938), *The Witness* (1955) and *My Mind* (1964).

My Mind

My mind is a lake;
come and row your boat in it.
I will hug your white shadow
and break into jewels against your sides.

My mind is a candlelight;
please close the window for me.
I will burn myself, quiet, to the last drop
trembling by your silken dress.

My mind is a wanderer;
play on your flute for me.
I will stay the quiet night through
listening to your tunes under the moon.

My mind is a falling leaf;
let me stay in your garden awhile.
I will leave you as a lonely wanderer
when the wind rises again.

The Banana Plant

How long since you left your native soil?
You must dream a pitiful dream.

Burning sick for home in the south
your soul seems lonelier than a nun.

O passionate woman craving for a shower.
I draw water from a well-spring to douse your feet.

Night gets cold now;
I will let you stay by my bed.

And I will be your willing servant.
Let us shelter from winter in the warmth of your silken skirt.

KIM, Sowol (1902-1934). Better known by his pen name Sowol, Kim, Chongshik was born in Kwaksan, North Pyong-an province, North Korea. As early as 1920 when he was 17, his genius manifested itself in a series of poems such as "*Flowers in the Mountains*", "*A Spring Traveler*" and others which appears in Ch'angjo (Creation). They were followed by another string of lyrical gems including "*The Azaleas*". Practically all of his work, about 250 pieces know so far, were written in a period of five years in and after 1920. His books are **Azaleas** (1925) and **Selected Poems** (1939).

The Azaleas

If you go away
because you cannot bear with me
in silence I bid you Godspeed.

Azaleas aflame on Yaksan Hill*
I will gather with full hands
and scatter them in your path.

Tread with a tread,
light and gentle,
on the flowers as you go.

If you go away
because you cannot bear with me,
no tears will I weep though I perish.

* A scenic spot noted for azaleas in the far north of North Korea

Song by the Brook

Were you born a wind
you might brush my lapels in the empty
plain where a brook runs, moonbeamed.

Were you born a slug
we might dream together, though idle,
on a mountain pass in the rainy night.

Were you born a stone
on the cliffs washed by the waves
I would hug you to roll into the sea below.

Were I a flame-spirit
I could burn your heart all night
till both of us turn to ashes.

Flowers in the Mountains

Flowers bloom
in the mountains;
spring, summer and autumn through
flowers bloom.

In the mountains
far and near
flowers bloom,
way up and apart in solitude.

Little birds carol
in the mountains;
they live in the mountains
for the love of flowers.

Flowers fade
in the mountains;
spring, summer and autumn through
flowers fade.

Gift of Love

These tears that fall for love's sake,
these pearl-like tears,
I wish to string them together
with an imperishable red thread
for her to wear around her neck
as a gift of love.

KIM, Yongnang (1903-1950). Born in Kangjin, South Cholla province, Kim went to Aoyama Academy in Japan, where he studied English. His first poems came out in **Shimunhak** (Poetry & Literature) in the thirties. He seriously considered poetry as an art expressing the beauty of experience. He had a successful effort to polish the Korean language to serve his purpose. A stray bullet ended his life during the Korean war in 1950. His works include *Collected Poems* (1935) and *Selected Poems* (1949).

Till The Peonies Bloom

I will await my spring
till the peonies bloom.
When the peonies drop their dead
I will mourn over the loss of spring.

One hot summer's day in May
when all the peonies are gone,
their petals glued to the ground,
my soaring desire crumbles to dust.

With my peonies gone my whole years end
and I shall drown in sorrow the rest of the year.
I will await my spring, glorious yet sad,
till the peonies bloom again.

May

A path from the field ends in a flowering village.
A lane out of the village opens to the greening field.
Endless rows of crops wave in the wind;
The sunlight slants upon each row,
Barleys exposing their fat waists.
Their wings untried, the fledgling orioles
Chase each other for the exercise of love-making.
The bright country lane blinds the eyes.
O mountain peaks, preened and coquettish,
Would you be gone somewhere for the night?

PARK, Yongchol (1904-1938). Born in Kwangju, South Cholla province, Park studied German literature at Tokyo University of Foreign Studies, Japan. Affiliated with **Haeoemunhakpa** (The Overseas Literature Group) he stood up for the purity and independence of art against the politically-oriented leftist literature. His pure lyrics movement made a turning point in the history of modern Korean poetry, but ironically his own poems lacked music and lyricism. **The Complete Works** came out in 1939, one year after his death.

The Departing Boat

I must go too
lest my youth be wasted
in tears.
I must go now.

How should I leave this sheltered harbor so easily?
Those peaks and ravines familiar to my feet,
those wrinkled faces dear to my heart
stay in my sight misty with tears.

Those who leave will miss those left behind;
isn't it what a fugitive feels like?
The wind blows the cloud adrift as I turn around.
Is there a shore for my landing?

I must go too
lest my youth be wasted
in tears.
I must go now.

YI, Yuksa (1904-1944). A native of Andong, North Kyongsang province, better known by his pseudonym, his real name being Yi Hwal, Yi went to Beijing University, where he studied sociology. His underground movement for Korean independence brought him into jail and death. **Collected Poems** was posthumously published in 1946.

The Grapes

Come July in my native village
grapes ripen into fruitfulness.

The legend of the village
hangs in clusters on the vines.
The dreamy sky in the distance
comes to be embedded in each grape.

When the sky-blue sea above
bares her breasts and a white sailboat
comes gracefully to the shore
the guest dear to my heart will arrive,
way-worn, in a blue robe.

If he comes to relish these fruit
why should I mind wetting my hands?

Boy, go and bring on the table
a silver tray and a clean calico napkin.

The Vertex

Gashed by the slashings of a harsh season
I was at last driven to the north,

where the bored heaven succumbed to the height
and the black frost cut my flesh.

I do not know where to stretch my leg;
where to land a single step.

No choice but to close my eyes and muse:
The winter here is a steel rainbow.

Wilderness

In the beginning of time
when heaven was first made
hardly was there any cockcrow.

When all the mountain-ranges
rolled seaward in love
they dared not to violate this place.

Through eons of time
the busy seasons flowered and faded
until a big river sprang into flowing.

Snow falling, a whiff of fragrance floats
from plum blossoms somewhere around;
I sow the seeds of my humble song.

In eons of time hence
a superman will come on a prancing white horse.
Let him chant my song to echo in this wilderness.

SHIN, Sokchong (1907-1974). Born of a family of literary tradition in Puan, North Cholla province, Shin followed his family to a remote village in the countryside where he spent his boyhood unmolested by the Japanese colonialists. His family suffered impoverishment, but he was richly rewarded with natural surroundings. **The Candlelight**, his first book of poems, won him a special position as a pastoral poet. After the liberation he could no longer remain in the quiet of pastoral firmness. **The Glacier** (1956) shows him keeping in touch with everyday world. His other books are **The Sad Pastoral** (1947), **Mountain Overtures** (1967), and **Soughing in the Bamboo Grove** (1979), posthumously published.

If You Call

If you call
I will come to you
like yellow ginkgo leaves
that drift by the autumn wind.

If you call
I will come to you
like a new moon that goes down
quietly at night when mist settles over the lake.

If you call
I will come to you
like a stream that winds its way
onto the sky-edge on mild spring day.

If you call
I will come to you
like the early spring sun that bathes the lawn
when white herons sing in the blue sky.

From Your Eyes

From your eyes
   the fresh green of May
   releases a sweet scent of white wild roses.

From your eyes
   the twinkling stars
   spin out their tales.

From your eyes
  the sound of a bell rings
  resonating from far away.

From your eyes
  the gentle hands wave a promise
  of reunion in far-off days.

From your eyes
  joyful days will come
  when we can share our happy stories.

It is Not Time Yet to Light the Candle

The slant rays of the setting sun feel sorry.
Mother, it is not time yet to light the candle.
Aren't the little birds of my mediation
still flying in the blue savannah of sky?
When the sky turns apple-red
those little birds will return with dusk;
our little lambs on the slope lie down
on the old green couch to bask in the lingering sun.
At last evening fog settles on the serene lake.
But, Mother, it's not time yet to light the candle,
for the old hill's meditative face hasn't faded yet;
one can hardly hear night's footfalls or its ebon
skirt rustling against its own feet as it emerges
from the far-off forest.
The sound of waves lapping against the dike dies away;
no wonder the crows visiting the country in late fall
have fled far away with the wind.
Now on your back the baby turns in his sleep
as if to ask you to hum him to sleep again.
Mother, do not light the candle yet.
You will see a tiny star glittering
in the sky beyond the timberline in the distance.

KIM. Kwangsop (1905-1977). Born in Kyongsong, North Hamgyong province, North Korea, Kim majored in English at Waseda University, Japan. Affiliated with The Overseas Literature school in the early 1930's, he began his literary career by introducing to Korea overseas literature in translation. Like many of his contemporaries, he published his poems in **Shiwon** (Poetry Garden). His early poems epitomize the general mood of the age against the backdrop of suffering and despair. His books are **Longing** (1938), **Heart** (1949), **The Sunflower** (1958), **The Dove at Songbukdong** (1969) and **Social Reaction** (1972).

The Dove in Songbukdong*

* Once a suburban area of Seoul

The city growing fast with a new lot number assigned
to the hilly suburban area of Songbukdong, the dove,
its native, has forfeited its residence.
Constantly scared by the explosions from a quarry
its heart has been cracked, run down.
And still it wings in a circle over its old habitat,
over the community against the blue morning sky
fresh as God's square
as if to bring blissful word to the people.
In the barren hillside in Sungbukdong region
no patch of ground is left for the bird
on which to land and peck a grain or two.
Wherever it turns
it can hardly escape the explosions
blowing up rock-mass in the quarry
and it has finally turned to a rooftop for shelter.
Driven by nostalgic urge at the sight of curling smoke
it wings back to the quarry assigned a lot number Hill I
to dip its bill in the warmth of a rock
that's just been split apart.
Once it looked upon man as a saint.
Friendly to man the bird loved as he did;
like man it enjoyed freedom.
Once the symbol of love and peace,
it has forfeited its hilly abode and man at the same time
and is left incapable of remembering
the very idea of love and peace.

Pathos

The sea at night is endlessly dark.
A light glimmers in the dead center.

The waves break against the boulders under my feet.
Freedom echoes eternal sadness in this land.

The gulls' crying through the darkness far away
laps on my ears and dies, ripping anew my heart's wound.

O bird of poetry that weeps while winging,
since you are fated to fly chartless in the darkness
let the sorrow-chained poet go with you
to the sea of the night.

YU, Ch'ihwan (1908-1967). Born in Ch'ungmu, South Kyongsang province, Yu left Yonsei University without a degree. During World War II he wandered in Manchuria. On liberation in 1945 he returned home to work as principal at a high school. His poems are tinged with metaphysical ponderings over life and nature. The incantatory tone of his poems fascinates the sensitive ear. His works include **Selected Poems** (1939), **Collected Poems** (1945), **Life Chapter** (1947), **Journal of a Blue Dragon Fly** (1949), and **The 9th Collected Poems** (1957).

Flag

It is a voiceless shouting,
a handkerchief of eternal nostalgic drive
waving into the distant blue of ocean.
Lofty mind flaps, wave-like, in the wind.
Grief spreads its wings like a heron
on the staff of thought, pure and upright.
I wonder
who first hoisted this aching heart
of ours into the air.

Rock

When I die, I shall be a rock.
Love and pity shall not touch,
nor joy nor anger ever moves me.
Exposed to the slashings of weather
I will whip myself to withdraw inward
in eternal, impersonal silence
until life itself is lost to memory:
drifting clouds, distant thunder.
No song will I ever sing
even in dreams
nor will I weep in pain
though split in two.
I shall be a rock when I die.

Life

Seeing the infinite world
caught in a grain of sand
and the eternal ups and downs
of human fate
I know my life is a mere cipher
in the immensity of the universe.
To live is a mere nothingness
And yet it is a simple joy.

The Isle of Ulung*

Shall I rise and go to the Isle of Ulung that lies,
dot-like, far out east beyond the sealine?

The rolling ranges of Mt. Changbeak
carpeting the land in beauty
must have sprung into being
the youngest favorite of the country.

Against the curling waves of the boundless sea
it floats in fear of being lost any minute;
it streams its hair of thought washed clean in the indigo wind
from the East Sea.

Gripped by a permanent longing for the land,
by an unending craving for the shore,
it seems to drift shoreward
pummelled forever by the waves and winds.

The moment it hears of anything undesirable
troubling the mainland in the remote distance
it beats its boyish breast
for the land lies helplessly out of its reach.

Shall I rise and go to the Isle of Ulung that lies,
dot-like, far out east beyond the sealine?

* 72 square kilometers in area, the island is located 40km east of North Kyongsang
province, serving as the easternmost outpost of Korea.

KIM, Kirim (1909-19??). Born in Songjin, North Hamgyong province, North Korea, Kim studied English at Tokyo University, Japan. He was the first to champion the modernist movement in Korea. He was reported missing during the Korean War, possibly forced to North Korea. He taught at college before the war. His books are **The Sun's Custom** (1936), **The Weather Chart** (1939) and **The Sea and the Butterfly** (1949).

The Sea and the Butterfly

Since no one has ever told her
how deep the sea is
the white butterfly has
no fear of the sea.

She lands on the sea taking it
for a patch of blue radish;
she comes home like a princess,
her wings wet in the salt waves.

In the month of March the sea doesn't bloom
and the pale moon chills the thin waist
of the sad butterfly.

Homesickness

Way beyond the mountains and clouds
nestles m y home village where there's
often a rumor about what's going on
in Russia across the border.

Suddenly, I stop short to hear
in the evening wind that rustles
in the roadside trees
someone calling a calf home.

Spring

April at last wakes up
like a lazy leopard,
glittering,
itching for motion,
blood-curdling,
and arching its back
before it strides over the winter.

SHIN, Sokch'o (1909-1976). Born in Hansan, South Ch'ungchong province, Shin studied philosophy at Hosei University, Japan. His early poems show Valerian influence. Later he turned to Taoist thoughts in search of classical form and poetics. Still later he absorbed Buddhist ideas into his work. His books include **Collected Poems** (1946), **The Gong Dance** (1959) and **The Song of Storm** (1970).

The Gong Dance *

* A Buddhist ritual dance performed by a monk or nun while striking a brass gong set up on the floor.

''Pleasure vanished like morning dew.'' - Siddhartha -

Despite my lifelong wish to live
like an immaculate petal
what shall I do
with the doleful fountain
that wells out
from the deep woods of my heart?

Perhaps it seems like the sound of a bell
bonging from a remote temple in the green mountains.
The bright moon is beaming idly
on the empty temple;
a sleepless philomel weeps sadly
on a spray in the back yard.
Woe is me! What shall I do?
How I've been dreaming
of the Nirvana
of matchless joy
that I can keep to myself!
Nevertheless,
dizzying dust has gathered unawares
on the clean mirror of my mind.

Flesh is sad.
A fault-ridden body of this temporary world.
The madding passion of this world
grips my body like a beast.
O this form, in such beauty!
In my treasure woods there's a path
running forever split between mind
and its enthralling body
where a hidden serpent wriggles.
Like a drifting cloud

quietly flows a stream
on which ripple down fallen petals.
How the rolling waters break into jewels!
What can ever stay the mighty flowing
before the stream empties into the blue sea?
How I envy that stream which flows freely at will!
Plum-blossoms blooming white
under the moon,
I lie down alone
in nun's quarters
but I can hardly get to sleep
as if laden with cares.

O dizzying concerns of this world!
What resignation for show!
Are the eight commandments and hymn for nothing?
O fruits of illusion born of human fate!
In the white jade skin hidden from sight,
lies the sad abyss of soul
I dream of.
O honeyed dew on the petals!
O heart-rending rapids
that rush down out of control!
O well-spring of my heart
that runs forever undrained!

So fleeting are the cataracts of flowers.
There's a sobbing in my beautiful ravine;
on the quiet flow of my frame,
on the dashing currents of mutability
I shall end in drifting
futilely like fallen petals.

Is it this very suffering flesh
that is only real?
This very self that exists for a brief spell,
this frame that flows flooded with the use of life,
a mere flowerbud that burns with pure desire,
an illusory butterfly worn with cares.

Far from the dust of this wide world
I have my eyebrows slightly arched
under my hood, tilted low.
This green shaded robe is kept spotless

free from a patch of shame.
The empty hill lies dotted with lilies
that ail in secret;
arrowroots running wild,
the moon shines brightly.
In the dead of the night
in the quiet of my upper room
I hear nothing but the dinning sound of water.
No other soul in sight but a lone candlelight
by which my neck band and my long-sleeved robe
are shed to ripple into a long-drawn sigh.
Like a dancing moth drawn to a flame
I chase a dream, sweet and endless.

Alas! Does solitude sire
a sinful serpent of thought?
O Maya that rises in quietness from the deep of my mind!
O dreaming Maya that rises inwardly!

On the myriad-folded ranges of mountains
arrowroots, twined and tangled,
run wild and free to wrap tightly
around an alder, slim and straight.
Are men also born to live tangled
and free like this?
For me
I have no wish nor attachment left in me
for I am a mere flower that blooms by nature.
This frame of mine that has grown big
charmed by the full-blown blossoms,
a sheer mass of roses.
Behold the hill where peach and plum blossoms
swirl in midair.

O seeds of evil chained to the eight phases of being!
How hard to cut off the stubborn affinity
clinging to the three worlds! *
I wish to wander madly in the dream woods
assigned to me for a living
but I do not know whither to go
like a sailor beaten unconscious by the storm.

* The world of desire-ridden beings, the world of beings with form, and the world of beings without form.

O my Bodhisattva,
Bodhisattva!
Save us, gracious Bodhisattva.
Save us, merciful Bodhisattva.
Save us, compassionate Bodhisattva.

Under the dome of boundless universe,
under the dome of boundless cosmos
my body is but a flower that blooms and blasts.
I wish to live sheltered in the cloud-capped mountains,
sheltered in the cloud-capped mountains.
And yet, and yet,
I still dream of the temporal world,
fascinated by the demon.

O demon, O demon,
wild beast of worldly passions!
Caged in a tile-roofed dungeon,
face to face with a cold gilded image
I write prostrate on the floor,
captive to the agony of this world;
the fire flaring up under my sable robe
is like incense that curls up
from a flowery fumigator.

In the small hours of the night when wind-bells
tinkle faintly in the wayward wind,
flowering sprays sway in a dance
against the casement of the abbot's quarters;
night seems deepening still;
the very canes doze in the cloud yard.
Left alone to myself in the cold of a cell
I quietly shed my long-sleeved robe;
rumpled in folds on the floor
it resembles a lotus-bloom
that floats on the blue water in a pond.

Can I get to sleep if I lie down
or dispel sadness if I sit to rest?
I stay up all night couching in the woods
of withering worries.
The road to the West chills me even in dreams;
mist darkens the vale coated with eons of time.
Where is paradise?
I do not so much as know whither I am going.

O Enlightened One, born of exalted Brahman,
how your mind illumines like gold!
The ocean-wide mercy of yours,
the lily-tender touch of yours.
Oh, the desire of flesh sucked into the region
of honeyed oblivion.
Look how the cataract tumbles a thousand feet
down to the cloud-thick pond.

Let me go along
all the miseries of this world
loaded on the back of my soul.

Shall I throw a surplice around my shoulders
around my shoulders to dance
while I strike the gong?
Shall I throw a surplice around my shoulders,
around my shoulders to lay me down
and hold the wanton moon that's slipped out of clouds
in the folds of my robe that drapes loose my empty heart?
I only wish to go in peace through this painful night,
through this painful night.

Alas, am I mad?
Or have I become a beast?
A beast of the demon?
Or a lustful doe descended to this world?
Woe is me. I must be mad.
Let me shake off temptation.
Pleasure vanished like morning dew.
O dizzying thoughts!
False senses!
Open sandy fields
rolling in and out by the waves!
The wind of regret blowing,
my heart goes hollow like a cave.
On the hillslope where flowers wilt
weeps a philomel
whose songs alone
mingle mournfully in the sound of flowing waters
rending the heart of a sleepless soul.

I push the window open to the moon,
its halo rimming hazily around the tinted clouds.

The moon is moored low
over the roof-edge that tilts heavenward;
verdant hills high and low enwrap me.
And all around is nil in dead quiet.
O Nightingale, you weeping philomel,
in what part of the clouds are you crying
throughout the night?
The sound of rushing waters seems
choked with sorrow, muffled by your cry.

Way off in the bushes by the brook
I undress myself and lave my fair body.
The empty hill and the moon shattered in the water
sail afloat down the gilded surface of the water.
Fair is its image sunk in the shallows;
a string of cream-white jewels scattered on the water-glass
only to gather into shape.
Unable to stay inside the cloud-rim
like the moon sunk into the water.

Bubble-like mountains locked in form.
I have come this far
to wash myself clean of the dust of sin.
Silence settles like a green veil;
in the spectacular beauty of the glittering image
the latent force of illusion comes to surface.
Alas!
Are mind and body at war everlastingly?
How the form of concept remains forever undefined!

O water! O flowing water! O overflowing water!
What a bliss that your body is broken loose!
Never to be hardened into form, your body is free
from worldly desires and sorrow.
Down the jewel vale that spokes in myriad directions
you flow freely out of the deep mountains
as the prime cause of lasting freshness,
as the pure fount that goes forever unpolluted.

Gong,
goes the bell at dawn;
night is about to end.
Gong, gong, goes the bell.
The peal of the bell rolls in waves
to echo the flowing water.

Look. I stand upright in the clean wash of glass.
What a lonely being I am!
Dawn brings all into their distinct form,
taking substance apart from image.
The moon casts a dim shadow
on the purpling woods.
The blue heaven lightening,
green peaks come near like a tower.
The crags shooting up through the clouds
and ever-vegetating trees
all come to life from the darkness,
giving off immortal light.
May you stay with me forever.
From the blue peaks up in the distance
comes in a surge an ocean of bright woods,
the thick forest flapping its gilded wings.
The morning sun spreads like roses about to open
and the birds asleep on the twigs
wake up to warble in joyous notes.

Ding, ding, beats the drum
Ding, ding, dong, beats the drum for the morning rite.
''Merciful Buddha'' intone the prayer.
In robe and prayer beads strung around my neck
I perform rites for the morning.
O horde that bows to an idol!
O sad hypocrites!
O false female believers!

Sound of drum   sound of prayer
Sound of prayer   sound of water
sound of water   sound of gong
sound of gong   sound of water
The sound of water flows
to ring the bell in waves.

In the countless columns of cloud
echoes the sound of the mountains.
The gentle wind that unlocks my heart
now passes through the rose bush
that carpets the slopes of remote mountains.
Letting my sleeves flow loose
I come down from the quiet of the temple;
I come down from the worthless vale of sorrow.

Flute

How sad, cold moon!
Do you set to no purpose
your remote dreams adrift
onto the hazy ancient sky
over the capital city?

Days and months have rolled
in and out since antiquity;
O moon, can't you end
the whirligig of life-storms?

I wonder if a master musician
could play on you, o flute,
to sweep away with your cosmic music
the clouds lowering over the blue ocean.

Over the ruins of decayed royalty
the cold moon and haze reign.
O heart-breaking flute of silence!

Catapulting a Stone

Onto the ocean
onto the infinite waves
I catapult a stone
as if to shoot an arrow into a void.

The stone flashes golden
as it raises a brief water spray
and vanishes.

O ocean,
where did you hide my arrow?

In the ocean
the infinite waves alone
roll for endless miles.

YI, Sang (1910-1938). Born in Seoul, Yi studied architecture at high school. Yi Sang is actually the pseudonym of Kim Haegyong. Because of t.b., he quit his position as architect and launched into a disorderly life; the so-called fin-de-siecle malady struck him. His behavior as well as his writing against convention came as a shock to his contemporaries. He was the first to employ the surrealistic technique rooted in psychological realism in Korean poetry. His books are **A Crow-s-eye-view** (1934) and **The Complete Works**, posthumously published.

The Mirror

There is no sound in the mirror;
perhaps no other world is that quiet.
I have ears also in the mirror,
the two pitiful ears unable to hear my own voice.
The I in the mirror is left-handed, a left-hander
incapable of a handshake. Though I cannot touch myself
in the mirror because of the mirror, how could I ever think of
meeting myself in the mirror but for the mirror?
I have no mirror with me now but there is always
the I in the mirror.
I do not know for sure, but the mirror I is absorbed
in his one-sided struggle.
The mirror I is my reversal. The resemblance
of the two is remarkable enough. I feel very sorry
that I cannot examine nor take care of myself in the mirror.

Flower-tree

In the midst of wilderness there stands a flower tree,
with no other tree near it. It blossoms in earnest as much as it years
in earnest for its companion somewhere.
And yet it cannot get to its fellow tree it is so much
in love with. I run away toward another tree as if I were
the very flower tree.

KIM, Kwanggun (1912-). Born in Kaesong, North Korea, Kim is one of the most faithful adherents of Kim, Kirim in championing the modernist movement in poetry. Affiliated with **Shi-inburak** (Poets' Village) he made a better success with his word-painting than his predecessor. His works include **Gaslight** (1939), **The Port of Call** (1947), **A Twilight Song** (1960) and **Gaslight** (1991), collected poems.

Lyricism of an Autumn Day

Fallen leaves are the banknotes of the Polish government-in-exile.
They remind me of an autumn sky spread over the bombed city of
Turon.
The road like a rumpled necktie
Fades into the cataracts of sunlight.
The 2 p.m. express races across the fields
Puffing cigarette smoke into the air.
The factory roofs flash their teeth
Between the ribs of poplar trees.
Beneath a cellophane cloud
A crooked wire fence sways in the wind.
Kicking through the grass alive with chirping insects
I throw a stone into the air as if to shake
the desolate thoughts off my chest;
It sinks, drawing a parabola, beyond
The screen of a slanting landscape.

Snowy Night

Snow drifts noiselessly in the middle of the night,
as if fetching me a glad message from afar.
A paper lantern burns low under the eaves.
Snow falls like a sad memory.
My breath condenses white upon my breast
as if a sigh issued from agony.
I light a lamp in the hollow of my heart;
I hear far off as I sail alone into the garden.

Snow drifts in the dark
Like so many slices of forgotten memory
Rousing in me a cold remorse and remembrance.
With no thread of light or whiff of scent around
I am left alone in a sombre garment
And my grief quietly settles
Upon the snow piling up endlessly.

Gaslight

The pale gaslight hangs in the empty sky.
Where does it signal me to go?
The long summer day hastens to fold its feathers.
Rows of towering buildings dip into the sunset
glow, like dull grave stones.
The loud nightscape makes a mass of confusion
Like rioting weeds.
Thought becomes dumb, lost to utterance.
The darkness brushes my skin.
The shouting in a street brings me
to tears, strange.

Dissolved into the flow of the empty crown
I know not why the lengthening shadow
Darkens like hell
As if I had caused the weight of grief.
The guidepost,
Where and how do you want me to go?
The pale gaslight hangs on the empty sky.

KIM, Hyonsung (1913-1976). Born in Pyongyang, North Korea and brought up in Kwangju, South Cholla province, Kim studied at Sungsil College. His poems are divided into three periods: the first concerned with the physical world, the second with a search for the inner world and the third with the theme of loneliness as an essential part of human existence. His works include **Selected Poems** (1957), **A Defender's Song** (1963), **The Solid Solitude** (1968), **The Absolute Solitude** (1970) and **The Complete Works** (1974).

Tears

Now and then
I wish to be a little life
that drips into the rich soil.

Tears,
flawless, untainted and pure,
are all that I possess.

Urged to surrender anything
more precious,
I have nothing left in me but tears.

As you load fruit on the boughs
seeing the fair blossoms gone,
so give me tears
as you have given me a laugh.

Prayer in Autumn

Let me pray alone in autumn.
Make me rich with your gift,
the humble mother tongue,
when leaves start to fall.

Let me love alone in autumn;
choose but one single soul.
Let me fertilize this hour
to bear the choice fruit.

Let me alone
so that my soul may have peace
like a bird that rests on a dry twig
after crossing the swelling ocean
and the valleys of lilies.

The Absolute Solitude

Now at last I've come to touch
the remote edge of eternity

On that edge I rub my eyes
to awake from my long sleep

From my fingertips,
the everlasting stars scatter, their light
gone from my fingertips,
I feel anew the body heat
that comes ever closer to me

Through this heat
I alone embrace the eternity
that ends in me

And from my fingertips
I set adrift like so much dust
the wings of my words lined with soft dreams

I stroke time and gain
with my wrinkled hands
the beautiful eternity that ends in me

And at my fingertips that can reach no further
I keep silent in the end, with my own poems.

NO, Ch'ongmyong (1913-1957). Born in Changyon, Hwanghae province, North Korea, No began writing while a student at Ehwa Women's University. Affiliated with **Shiwon** (Poetry Garden), No made herself conspicuous as a rare talent. She made her solitude and self-torture a weapon against the hostile universe. *The Coral Reefs* (1938) finds her drowned in fond reminiscences. *The Song of Deer* (1959), posthumously published, shows her outgrowing her nettling solitude on the way into the world of love and repentance.

Watching the Stars

As a tree tilts heavenward
so we must go watching the stars overhead
though our feet kick dust on the ground.
What if you should be ranked
higher than the next fellow?
What if your name should be made
greater than those of others?
What if you should be revenged on your enemy?
All end in trifles
not worth a penny for a drink.
We must go ahead watching the stars overhead
though our feet kick dust on the ground.

Deer

That long neck of yours
makes you a sad creature.

Always quiet and gentle
with the scented crown
you must come of a noble tribe.

Watching your own image
mirrored in the stream
you like to recall the lost legend.

Lost in irresistible nostalgia
you crane your sad neck
to gaze at the far-away hills.

Behind Prison Bars

I hear a dog barking.
It cheers me up like a familiar voice.
Certainly someone lives near.

I hear a dog barking,
a reminder of a happy family
shoes arranged neatly in the doorway.

In the early morning
kitchen gets warm with cooking steam.
Soup sizzles over the brazier.
Who cares if grandmother complains?
The dog's barking at dawn
transmits a breath of hearth and home.
The world outside is pure happiness
to those dumped behind the prison bars.

SO, Chongju (1915-). Born in Sunchang, North Cholla province, So went to Buddhist College, where he studied Buddhism. Well-known by his pen name Midang, he is considered the dean of contemporary Korean poets. **The Snake**, his first book of poems, came out in 1941. In 1940, he left for Manchuria, where he led a wanderer's life before returning home on liberation in 1945. So's basic philosophy of art is rooted in aestheticism. His magic manipulation of language and his superb use of the evocative power couched in Korean sentiments make him a rare talent in the whole gamut of modern Korean poetry. His books are **The Snake** (1941), **The Nightingale** (1948), **Selected Poems** (1956) and **Blue Days** (1991), selected poems.

Beside the Chrysanthemum

For a chrysanthemum to bloom
the cuckoo must have been crying
that long since springtime.

For a chrysanthemum to bloom
the thunder must have roared
aloud in the dark clouds.

How dearly you remind me of my sister
who stands before her mirror
now back from wandering far in the alley
of her youth full of yearning and wistfulness!

For your golden petals to unfold
it frosted so hard last night
I had to spend sleepless hours.

The Winter Sky

I have rinsed clean
in the dream of millennial nights
the exquisite eyebrows of my beloved
enshrined in the recess of my heart
and transplanted them in the heaven;
the most ferocious bird on the wing in mid-winter
passes at a cautious distance
from the eyebrows of fearful beauty.

The Nightingale Path

Tears glinting in beads
when azaleas shower down their petals
my beloved has gone away from me playing
on the flute a thousand miles to the far West.
Adjusting her cotton dress again and again
my beloved has gone away a thousand miles
to China, the way of no return.
I should have woven for her my sad story
into a pair of fine-hempen sandals
or cut off with a sharp silver knife
my useless locks of hair to plait for her.
A paper lantern glowing, night sky stretched tired,
its throat wet in the curving galaxy in heaven
the nightingale strains out a heart-rending tune
as if drunk with its own blood.
O my beloved who has gone alone so far
away beyond the rim of the sky!

Looking at Mt. Mudung *

Poverty is a mere mask for rags and tatters,
for it cannot cover up our natural skin and mind,
which are constant as the summer mountains
that discloses its emerald green ridges in the bright sun.

As the green mountain feeds in secret orchids
and precious herbs on its lap, so we must
bring up our young ones.
In the afternoon when worries weigh us down,
A married couple in love will relax
now sitting together and then lying side by side;
wife regarding her man with love,
man caressing his woman on the forehead.

Even if thrown into the thornbush or into a ditch,
we will go with a belief that we shall endure
like hidden jewels with green moss richly gathered.

* The name of a mountain east of Kwangju in the south.

The Fresh Green

What shall I do?
I've fallen in love,
in secret love.

Flowers have all faded;
the green breaks into flame again,
enfolding me again.

While red petals fall
and scatter in thick flakes,
in a sad gesture hard to bear.

They fall on the grass in the wind,
like a soft breath of an ancient maiden,
like her hair streaming in the wind.

They drift about again this year;
they tremble as they fall.

I've fallen in love,
madly in love,
too full to carol like a cuckoo.

PARK, Tujin (1916-). Born in Ansong, Kyonggi province, Park taught at Yonsei University until his retirement in 1981. His first poems were published in **Munjang** (Literary Composition) in 1936. He seeks his material in physical nature: mountains, trees, the sea, and the sun. He looks to nature for the salvation of corrupted humanity. Among his books are **The Blue Deer Poems** (1946), in collaboration with others, **The Sun** (1949), **Midday Prayer** (1953), **Selected Poems** (1956), **Alpine Plants** (1973), **Lives of Apostles** (1973), **Biography of Stone and Water** (1976) and **Autumn Cliffs** (1991), selected poems.

Hymn to the Graveyard

The round mounds of the dead in the graveyard
seem not that lonesome after all for they are
richly covered with beautiful turf.

The bleached bones will gleam in the darkness
of the grave and the death smell will be fragrant.

The dead who fed on sorrow while alive
will not be sad to be lying low; they long only
for the sun that will shine bright someday into the grave.

Red pasqueflowers bloom on the green turf;
mountain birds warble in the air; the dead lie silently
in the grave, warmed in the spring sun.

Before Thy Love

Shall I sit face to face with thee, Rabboni *,
whose words sparkle flame into my eyes?
Will the bleeding wounds on my toes and palms
and heart heal up, as I silently weep
in the vale baptized with thy blood?
The mocking ululation of beasts turns to music;
the falling head over heels from a cliff to a rhythmic motion.
If only I could swallow thy flame,
if only I could be whipped on the back by thee
my bitter tears would glisten iridescent like scales;
madness would become a rapturous rest.

* A Hebrew word meaning a teacher or a master.

The Sun

Rise, fair sun. Rise,
washed clean in your face.
Blaze up and devour the darkness all night through
behind the hills before you glow coal red
in your boyish face.

I abhor the moonlight.
How I abhor the night when the moon shines
on the tearful valley;
on the desert garden!

Rise, fair sun. Rise.
I adore the verdant hills in your company;
I love to see them flapping their wings.
In the presence of verdant hills,
I can hardly contain my joy, if left all alone.

I pursue a deer; I pursue him
onto the sunny hillside.
I will frolic with him if I catch him.
I will pursue a tiger, I will pursue a tiger
and play with him if I catch him.

Rise, fair sun. Rise.
When you rise, I will call aloud
for flowers and animals and birds
to gather around me
and I will live in peace and innocence
as in a dream.

The Youthful Sea

O sea, break as you pour down from heaven
O sea, break as you gush from earth
O sea, break with your waves pouring upon waves

Our love that falls apart
Our country that falls apart
This century that falls apart
You've swallowed them up as you roll
as if nothing had ever happened
With your blue jaws wide agape
You swallow up the fiery ball of sun
and the chunk of moon the shining chunk

One and all forever
Regardless of good or wicked
You assault our time yesterday today and tomorrow
Our dreams our pride and grief
dissolving them in your breast

And eternally you roll in and out
in an endless passion for infinite expanse
In blue as blue can be
With your will-power a thousand fathoms deep
In silence a thousand fathoms deep

PARK, Mogwol (1919-1978). A native of Kyongju, South Kyongsang province, Park's first poems were published in **Munjang** (Literary Composition) in 1939. Like two other members of the Blue Deer Group, he also turned to nature for his material. His world, however, is set against the backdrop of local legends and folklore. Adept in manipulating language in a simple vernacular tone, he succeeded in fusing sense and sound. His books include **The Blue Deer Poems** (1946), in collaboration with others, **The Mountain Peach Blossoms** (1946), **Orchids and Other Poems** (1959), **Sunny or Cloudy** (1964), **In the Darkened Window** (1969) and **Leaves Falling in Kyongsang Province** (1969).

The Traveler

Ferrying across the river
before he takes a path through

the wheatfields the traveler
moves like the moon in the clouds.

A single road stretches southward
three hundred leagues long.

The sunset glow tints every
village where wine matures.

The traveler moves like the moon
in the clouds.

April*

A solitary peak
where pine pollen drifts.

When an oriole complains
of the long April day,

The ranger's blind daughter
left to herself in her lone cabin

Presses her ear
against the doorpost.

* The original refers to the intercalary month of the lunar calendar.

48 ❧

Love

I am but a heart-broken dreamer,
a foolish dreamer.

There's a rock I polish in private
with my tears every night;

I polish the rock with my tears
the livelong night.

When ever will my love and heaven
be mirrored in this dark
and stubborn rock?

Lowering the Coffin

The coffin was lowered
into the heart's depth
as if anchored by a rope.
Lord, forgive him.
Placing the Bible at his head
I wished him goodbye
and hastened down the hill,
my clothes covered with dirt.

Since then
I have seen him in my dreams;
his long-jawed face turning round,
he called me "Brother"!
"Yes", I responded with all my might;
he could not have heard me, though.
Only I hear his voice
from this world
where snow and rain fall.

Where have you gone,
with your eyes, gentle, sad, and kind?
I hear your voice calling me
"Brother"!
yet my voice cannot reach you
from this world
where I can hear fruit drop with a thud.

YUN, Tongju (1917-1945). Born in Kanto, a border area between Korea and China, brought up among Korean patriots-in exile, Yun studied English at Rykkyo University, Japan, after a brief attendance in Yonsei University. Arrested by the Japanese police and put in jail on the charge of underground activities for Korean independence, he died in prison six months before the liberation. His works were published posthumously in 1950 under the title of **The Sky, the Wind, Stars and Poems**.

Counting the Stars

Up in the sky where seasons pass
autumn fills the air.
In this quietude
I could almost count those autumnal stars,
yet I may not count them off one by one,
because the dawn will soon break,
because I have still tomorrow night,
because my youth is not yet done.

One star for Memory
Another star for love
another for loneliness
another for longing
another for poetry
another for Mother, o mother.

Mother, I will call each star by name, lovely name,
names of school children with whom I shared a desk
names of foreign girls like P'ae, Kyong, Ok
names of girls who are now mothers,
names of my poor neighbors,
names of birds and beasts like dove, pup, rabbit, mule, deer,
names of poets like Francis James, Rainer Maria Rilke;
they are too far away
like the stars in the sky.
Mother, you are far away too
in the north.

Driven by yearning for what I cannot tell
I write my name down
on the starlit hillside
and cover it with earth.
Insects are chirping all night long
as if pitying my humble name.

When winter is gone and spring arrives
grass will green the hillside
where my name is buried
like green turf breaking out on the graves.

The Prologue

I wish my life to be led until death
without a patch of shame.
Under the scrutiny of heaven
I feel painfully hurt
by a single breath of wind
that stirs the leaves of grass.
I must love all things mortal
with a spirit to sing the stars;
I must follow the path destined to me;
Tonight as before wind rustles against the stars.

The Cross

The sunlight that has been chasing me
now hangs on the cross
on the rooftop of a church.
How could it have scaled
the steeple so high?

No bell is ringing;
I fool around giving a whistle.

Were I to be allowed the cross
as was Jesus Christ,
who suffered but was happy,

I would gladly hang my own head
and let my blood flow in quiet
like a flower that flares
under the darkening skies.

PARK, Namsu (1918-). Born in Pyongyang, North Korea, Park studied law at Chuo University, Japan. He launched his literary career with his first poems coming out in **Munjang** (Literary Composition) in 1939). He attaches great importance to the intellectual manipulation of language, maintaining that art is born when ideas fuse with artistry. He has taught at college before he emigrated to the U.S.A. in 1976. His books are **A Tavern** (1939), **A Paper Lantern** (1940), **Sketch of Seagulls** (1958), **Secret Burial of a Bird** (1970) and **Woods' Memory Nowhere** (1991).

Hands

The moment an object falls
the hand tilts up into the void.

How long has the hand
possessed and lost?

How briefly it possesses
volumes of emptiness!

When angry the hand
turns into a shaking fist.

When the fist relents
it turns into prayer.

How long has the hand been
seeking emptiness?

The final conviction the hand has gained is:
Nothing can indeed be within its grasp.

Birds

1
In the shoal of wind
churning up the skies,
in the shade of trees
rustling in a whisper,
the birds sing.
They do not know they sing.
They do not know they love.
A pair of birds, their bills
sunk in each others' plumes,
delight in the sharing of body heat.

2

The birds do sing
not for meaning;
they do love
not for pretension.

3

The hunter aims with a load of lead
at the essence of birds but
what he gains by shooting is
but a fallen body smeared with blood.

HWANG, Kumchan (1918-). Born in Sokcho, Kangwon province, and brought up in North Korea, Hwang came to the south in 1946. His writing career started early in 1946 but his major breakthrough came in 1952 through **Hyondae Munhak** (Modern Literature). His books include **Season's Romance** (1959), **The Spot** (1965), **The May Mountain** (1969), **The Afternoon Han River** (1971), **Cloud and Rock** (1975), **A Little House on the Hill** (1984), **Solitude, Nothingness, Love** (1986) and **Unforgettable though Parted Far from Home** (1991).

Candlelight

Candlelight.
No sooner has its wick
been ignited
it starts racing toward the end.

A frail resistance
against surging darkness.
From whom has it inherited
the spirit of silent sacrifice?

Fate, perhaps.
Unconscious of time-limit
since it came into existence.

It burns limited in time
it doesn't grieve
but enjoys every bit
of flowering moment
in a dance.

Prayer

Lord God,
a tiny soul has just left
for your land,
the soul of my little daughter Aeri.

Long illness
has wrecked her thin.
I fear if she could ever make
her long journey, safe.

Some may sin
out of luxury;
she has never sinned
even for fun.

My friends called her
an angel
on earth.

She's departed.
an eternal parting,
never to meet again on earth.

Lord God,
Keep me in your providence
so that I might see her again
in your land.

Lord God who loves
goodness in man,
please love the little soul more.

HAN, Ha'un (1919-1975). Born in Hamju, South Hamgyong province, North Korea, Han graduated from Beijing University, China. To his despair he found himself stricken with leprosy in his early twenties. He set about wandering in Manchuria before coming to the South in 1948. Han succeeded in sublimating into art his personal misery and bitter life experience as a leper and social outcast. Recovered later, he worked for the Korean Hansen Association. His works include **Selected Poems** (1948), **Oaten Pipe** (1957) and **Dirt Road** (1960).

Oaten Pipe

Fluting *filniriri*
I play on my oaten pipe
longing for the spring hills
and my old home village.

Fluting *filniriri*
I play on my oaten pipe
longing for the green flowering hills
and my childhood.

Fluting *filniriri*
I play on my oaten pipe
longing for the crowds of men
and human affairs.

Fluting *filniriri*
I play on my oaten pipe
wandering over valleys and crossing rivers;
weeping over hill after hill.

Blue Bird

When I shall die
and be no more
I will be
a blue bird

To fly freely about
in the azure sky
and over the green fields;

To sing a blue song
and cry
a blue cry.

KU, Sang (1919-). Born in Wonsan, South Hamgyong province, North Korea, Ku graduated from the Religion department of Nihon University, Japan. His first poems came out in the early forties before he escaped from the Communist regime to the south. Awardee of many literary prizes and member of the Korean Academy of Arts, Ku has published **Condensed Perfume** (n.d.), **Kusang** (1951) **Poems of the Burnt Earth** (1956), **The Reality of Language** (1980), **The Crow** (1981) and **Selected Poems** (1984).

War Poems 1

Out of the patched-glass window of boarded shacks
children's faces hang like a flaming sunflower.

The blinding sun beats upon them
to turn aside. I also turn aside.

The shadow about to wail follows me;
I stop mistakenly at a turning.

On the hedge in a heap of ashes
forsythias are about to unfold.

Chenny races down the hillslope,
her front teeth all out.

I become jolly as if drunk;
shadow overtakes me with a smile.

War Poems 7

O rows and rows of mounds for the dead!
They may not rest here in peace.

Until only yesterday we aimed our guns
at your lives and now with the same hands
that pulled the trigger we have collected
the torn flesh and broken bones
to bury in the sunny hillside
with turf covered.

Death seems more generous
than love and hate.

From where we stand, your spirits and I,
our hometown is not far - only
30 *li* beyond the border.

The desert of this desolate ridge
loads me down like heaviness itself.

While alive you and I were bound by hate.
Now that you are dead your lingering regret
gets imbedded into my desire.

Up in the sky that seems to touch the earth
the clouds drift to the north.

Sporadic reports of guns in the distance.
I wail over the graveyard
of love and hate.

Shame

At the Metropolitan Zoo.
I peek across the wire netting
behind the iron fence
intently looking for an inmate
which possibly possesses a sense of shame

Hello, manager, can you tell me
if there're any signs of it
on the flaming rear of an ape?

On the bear's paw, continually licked by its owner?
On the seal's moustache?
or on a female parakeet's beak?

I've come to the zoo
in search of a sense of shame
long since atrophied
in the populace of the city.

CHO, Chi-hun (1920-1968). Born in Yong-yang, North Kyongsang province, Cho graduated from Hehwa college, presently Sunggyn-gwan University. Affiliated with the Blue Deer group, he resorted to nature for his poetic setting. His nature is coated with the patina of history and polished with artifice. His works include **Mountain Rain** (1930), **The Blue Deer Poems** (1946), in collaboration with other members, **Grass Notes** (1952), **Selected Poems** (1956), **Before History** (1959), **Lingering Tones** (1964) and **Poems after Blue Deer Poems** (1968).

Falling Petals

If the petals are shed
should we blame the breeze?

The stars sparsely studded beyond the bamboo
screen fade out one by one.

In the wake of a nightingale's song
the far-away hills seems to draw near.

Should we blow out the candle
now that the petals are falling?

The falling petals cast
their shadows in the yard.

And the white papered sliding
door glows incarnadine.

Lest the beautiful soul
living in seclusion

Be known to the secular minds,
I have some misgivings.

When the petals fall in the morning
I wish to cry my heart out.

The Nun's Dance*

* A symbolic Buddhistic dance expressive of hardship and suffering every novice has to go through before attaining Enlightenment. The dance can be performed by the monk.

Folded delicately into shape,
the fine gauze white cowl lightly wavers.

The bluish head, shaved close,
is veiled under the flimsy cowl.

Her cheeks in a glow
grace her with grief.

The candle burns quietly in the empty hall
and the moon seeps into every paulownia leaf.

Her long sleeves billow up
against the vast heaven like wings outspread.
Her white socks no less match her movement.

She lifts her dark eyes to gaze
on a star in the far-off sky.

Her cheeks fair as peach blossoms
are stained with a tear-drop or two.
In the face of worldly cares
her agony beams like a starlight.

Her arms swaying and turning,
folding and unfolding tell
of her pious devotion at heart.

When the crickets chirp through the midnight
the fine gauze white cowl lightly wavers,
delicately folded into shape.

At Toriwon*

Once over, the heart-rending war
seems to strike us less painful than a gusty storm;
thatched houses lie gutted by fire
and huts caved in.

Sadness cutting into my heart I ramble
about the village razed to the ground.

Only a few soy jars stand
unharmed in heaven's grace.

I sense my own life has been spared
the way the earthenwares remain unscathed.

Soon the scattered villagers
gather onto the ruined site;
they just gaze on the far-away hills.

The sky spreads above the village
in the autumn sun

and those full-blow cosmoses
sway in the chill wind.

* A site of battle during the Korean war (1959-1953)

YI, Tongju (1920-1979). A native of Haenam, South Cholla province, Yi left Hehwa College without a degree. His first poems were published in **Munhak Yesul** (Literary Arts) in 1946. His work shows the natural flow of the vernacular compact with imagery typical of things Korean. His works include **Your Friend** (1946), **Bridal Night** (1951), **Gang-gang-suwolei** (1959), and **Folk Melody** (1979).

The Bride

Tongue-tied,
the ride brightens into a flower
at her own parents' home.
Once back to her in-laws
she metamorphoses into an obedient butterfly,
her lips sealed tight.

She bites her lips to wrap her tears
in the folds of her breast-tie.
Quietly turning around she lets her laugh
slip across the back of her modest hand.

When someone comes hemming into the house
she hurriedly trails her long skirt,
her hands folded in awe
and withdraws into her tiny shell;

she casts herself into a picture
framed half hidden at the door post.

She is a mother, kind and generous,
to a shrew-like sister of her husband.

Affection is bound by law;
she writes in a graceful court style
to her man who never comes back to her.

The bride, her hair tidy as a quill,
is now a mother, her hair turned silver;
she can hardly thread a needle, her sight dimmed.

Though her son is a floating cloud
she pins her hope on him
and calmly waits for him
while she awaits her own death.

Gang-gang-suwole*

Silver fish swarms into the rapids.
Petals scattered on the waters
whirl in a moon halo.

Gang-gang-suwole,
we never sing but sorrow arises.

In the white rose garden
a peacock dozes, spell-bound.

We'll leap and hop around
waltzing to the tunes of gang-gang-suwole.

Streaming ribbons wrap around the world;
long locks of hair encircle us all.

The moonshine tastes stronger
than wine when drenched in dew.

Flags are torn to pieces;
reeds are flattened.

Gang-gang-suwole,
Gang-gang-suwole.

* This is the chanted refrain of a circle folk dance. To reproduce the melody of the
original poem is practically impossible.

KIM, Suyong (1921-1969). Born in Seoul, Kim went to Yonsei University, where he studied English. His literary career started with **The New City and Citizens' Chorus**, an anthology in collaboration with two other poets. He was strongly committed to the society in which he lived. Another book **The Game** came out in 1959.

Grass

Grass lies flattened
leaning in the rain-driven east wind;
grass lies flattened
until it weeps.
Skies clouded, grass wept more
before it lies flattened again

Grass lies flattened before the wind does
weeps before the wind does
rises before the wind does

Skies clouded, grass lies flattened
flattened
ankle-deep
flattened sole-deep
though it lies flattened after the wind
it rises before the wind
though it weeps after the wind
it smiles before the wind
skies clouded, grass roots lies flattened before anything.

A Waterfall

It falls over the upright cliff
without a touch of fear.
A thing incapable of definition.
Without meaning to fall into any specific purpose
it falls incessantly like a noble spirit
day and night regardless of seasons.

When marigolds and houses fuse in the night darkness
it falls sounding upright sounds.

The upright sound sounds upright.
The upright sound summons another upright sound.

The water dropping like a bolt of lightning
affords no moment of intoxication;
it falls without a sense of height or width
as if capsizing stupor and stability.

CHO, Pyong-hwa (1921-). Born in Ansong, Kyonggi province, Cho studied physics and chemistry at Tokyo Superior Normal School. Undoubtedly the most prolific writer yet known, he has more than 20 volumes of poems to his credit. Simply stated, his poems make vignettes o f words on the everyday experiences of city life. His main theme is the lonely fate of man. Among his works are An **Undesirable Heritage** (1946), **One Day's Comfort** (1950), **Before Love Passes** (1955), **Night's Tale** (1963), **In Search of Time's Lodging** (1964), **The Osan Interchange** (1971), **Between Dust and Wind** (1972) and **Mother** (1973).

Empty as Death

Anything empty as death?
Anything futile as death?
Anything lonely as death?

Dismissing death when haughty as youth
Sentimental death transcended by youth
Stillness of death indifferent to youth.

Now bobbing up and down before
eyes hesitating
You and I
One leaving, the other left behind
at the point of parting

Listening to death
Looking death in the eyes
Looking at the neck of death

Anything frail as death?
Anything pitiful as death?
Anything silent as death?

Never to Meet Again

We are heading where there is no address
We are heading where there is no way
We are heading where there is no use for words
Cut off from ties to things of this world -
Tears, attachment, joy and suffering -
We are moving to where there is no address
Moving from this world visible

To that world invisible
Each one separately
From the other
day after day

KIM, Chongsam (1921-1984). Born in Unyul, Hwanghae province, North Korea, Kim went to a high school in Japan. His literary career started with his association with other poets in the 1950s. His poems are characterized by his tragic vision on life, history and the age he lives in. His books are **The Trio Anthology, War and Music and Hope** (1957), in collaboration with two other poets, **The Twelve Tone Scale** (1969), **School for Poets** (1977), **A Boy Drummer** (1979), **Somebody Asked Me** (1982) and **Peacefully** (1984).

The Salt Sea

I am as old and outworn as my shoes.
Someone has left his hut deserted,
whose roof is also old and outworn.
There is no drop of water.
Only a nameless peak reflects
the gleam of sunlight.
There's no single bird.
The salt sea contains nothing, no man,
no trace of water.
No fork of a road of death either.

When That Day Comes

I shall die sooner or later
in the mountains
or in highlands,
whatever the place.
I shall die
into a Mozart's flute note,
for I am not cut out for this world;
for I am ill.
I shall die soon
and be an infinite plain,
a floating cumulus,
or a boy that shepherds a flock of lambs.
I shall die soon.

A Bird

Every day almost at the same hour
just one little bird was chirping
in the same old tree.

The same as yesterday
thornbushes were aglow, three of them:

One was for mother's grave;
another
for a little brother's.

Every day almost at the same hour
just one little bird was chirping
in the same old tree.

KIM, Ch'unsu (1922-). Born in Ch'ungmu, South Kyongsang province, Kim studied Fine Arts at Nihon University, Japan. An outstanding critic as well as a poet, he used to teach at college. His books include **Cloud and Rose** (1948), **Swamp** (1950), **The Flag** (1951), **The Neighbor** (1953), **The First Collected Poems** (1954), **Sketch of Flowers** (1959), **The Death of a Girl in Budapest** (1969) and **Prelude for the Flower** (1991).

The Death of a Girl in Budapest

Winter is setting in across Eastern Europe,
ice filming over the Danube,
roadside trees starting to drop their dead at dusk
when suddenly half a dozen Soviet bullets
knocked you down,
more wretched than a rat dead in a ditch.
At the moment
your bashed head bounced into the air
for 30 seconds.
From your neck where your head had been
blood was gushing out to douse the pavement
so familiar to you when alive.
You're fourteen, as reported.
Over your death
not a single white dove flew;
Budapest's night could not weep
freely over your death.
Now freed at last through death
your soul would return to ride
the blue waves of the Danube,
way off from the watchful eyes
and weep aloud for those left behind you.
Is the Danube flowing quietly?
Does it run as sweetly as Johann Strauss's melodies?

Why is it that a 13-year-old Korean girl
should have died, so innocent,
on the mute sand of the Han river
that's not made famous in music
nor well marked on the world map?
Why should she have died, her hand
jerked into the hollow of the air,
with the devil laughing behind her back?
Why should she?

O girl in Budapest, what you've done
isn't done on your own, it seems,
for the death of a girl on the sands of the Han river
rends in bitterness the hearts of her people.
The angry river of memory will for certain
flow today and tomorrow
bringing tears to the eyes of the people,
to the eyes of the people.
Though the brave were gone and no more,
though your brothers and uncles fell
at the same gun that aimed at you
that river of memory will be flowing
through the conscience of mankind.
In the days when feckless Peters
deny three times before cockcrow
why should that man crucified to death
bring to mind all memories
on this sleepless night?

I was 22, in college,
thrown into jail in Tokyo
charged with being a reactionary Korean.
One day
I heard a voice, sickening voice,
issuing from my own throat.
''Mother, I wish to live.''
The voice I had never heard before
seemed to come from somewhere far away;
Then I battered my head against the concrete floor.
I could hardly resist wailing,
sorrow welling up within me.

Who could have made mockery of me?
Did my shame stem from my desire to live?
Did the death that Budapest girl had thrown herself into
sprout from the seeds of shame
sown in the hearts of those trembling before death?
The greening sprout does not spring
from the impersonal vegetation but
from the gushing blood of the girl
fallen in the fight for freedom.
The greening sprout shoots up in an image
that betrays our own cowardice;
it springs into blossom
through the nights, sleepless and anguished.

Man will fall but he will rise.
Man will fall again and again for ages
shuddering in the abyss of existence.
Man will continue to weep with the parents
who lost their daughter to the devils' bullets.

Winter was setting in across Eastern Europe,
ice filming over the Danube,
roadside trees starting to drop their dead at dusk,
when suddenly half a dozen Soviet bullets
knocked you down,
more wretched than a rat dead in a ditch.

CHONG, Hanmo (1923-1991). Born in Puyo, South Ch'ungchong province, Chong studied Korean at Seoul National University, where he taught for many years. His poems show a compact structure expressing lucid meaning. His first poems appeared in the 1950s in **Hyondae Munhak** (Modern Literature) and **Munye** (Literary Arts). He has published **Superfluity of Chaos** (1958), **Lyricism of Blank Space** (1959), **Baby's Room** (1970) and **Dawn** (1975).

Bird

O bird that flies about,
invisible,
in the far distance
of the lavender mist.

Rinsed in the sunrays
golden wings in a glitter
it glides across the sky;

Streaking
through the dark
and a clear voice of wind
vibrates my heart-strings.

A sudden awakening of dawn.
A bird flies far out
in the lavender of morning mist
glimmering in
and out of sight.

Late Autumn

Sorrow is eternally
silent as stone

Under the blank sky
about the fade

a cock calmly
folds its feathers

Like birds nosing cheerless
nestward, flowers gone,
people are heading homeward
cossetting their wind-swept hearts.

Parting

Now so beautiful
it sounds
high-pitched tone
of strings and wooden pipes

shrill voice of vocal exercise
a number of partings
that have fled in tremolo
bruises left in my heart

like ice cream flavor
taste of sorrow tingles my veins

upon the blue surface
of a rolling ocean
white petals waver to drift
and our parting comes to an end

to end is to rest at ease
or to pray in quietude

onto the burning lips
the moon halo ripples
as memory ripples in a ring

light on the window
blowing of a whistle
a white snow-road

pain squeezing the heart may
be a life burning itself
or dimly written words
washed out by streaming tears
or lingering perfume

now from afar
shaking in the wavering wind
beyond your reach
beyond mine
like a star in the sky

KIM, Kyudong (1923-). Born in Chongsong on the Tumen River, North Hamgyong province, North Korea, Kim attended Yonsei University Medical School. His first poems came out in **Yesul Choson** (Arts Korea) in 1948. In the early fifties (1951-1953), he was involved in the modernist movement in arts. He has published **Butterfly and Square** (1955), **The Present Myth** (1958), **The Hero Amid Death** (1977), **Clean Hope** (1990) and **Song of Life** (1991).

Mother's Letter from the North

In a dream you came,
you, who had suddenly left home at twenty-three,
came back a forty-seven-year-old traveler.
How I have been waiting to see you once in a lifetime!
Indeed, you came. How I've been worried about you
day in day out all these years!
You just cried, your face buried in my lap.
You cried and cried like a child,
cried your heart out.
You came back home, my dear boy, surviving
the passage of all these years, many far-off years.
And you said to me: ''I'll never leave home, Mother.''
Your eyes in tears
said it again and again.

Home

At home
there's no burning passion or the like.

The village nestles rounded by the mountains
and grow old with the mountains.

In the village a row of poplars,
seized by longing for the distant sea
rustle, sobbing in the skies.

By day the cocks in the neighboring village
flap their wings crying for the ancient times.

SHIN, Tongjip (1924-). A native of Taegu, North Kyongsang province, Shin graduated from Seoul National University, where he studied politics. He went to the U.S. for a research trip to Indiana University. A wardee of many literary prizes, Shin has published over a dozen books of poems. Among his works are **Banishment of Lyricism** (1954), **Another Prologue** (1958), **Seething Voice** (1965), **An Empty Cola Bottle** (1968), **The Man on Dawn** (1970), **Sending Message** (1973), **Wayfarer** (1975), **The Sea for Three Pesons** (1979) and **Selected Poems** (1980).

A Shoe

A scrap of iron jerks its arms upright
in the field where an odd shoe lies exhausted.
A cricket says Mass inside the shoe.
Its faint voice soon dies out
and silence soft-lands on the field awhile.
Grass blades swaying,
the shoe screams all of a sudden
in a voiceless shouting.
Come and listen,
the shoe is calling its mate.
Don't be misled anyway.
A worthless man's feet
are useless even after death.
Where is my mate gone?
The shoe is releasing nostalgia in a body.
The cricket resumes its prayer
in the dusk of autumn.

Vertigo

How long can man stare
into his own whirling center?
How can he endure the vertigo
The whirlpool engenders?
Eyes can no longer see anything
But the darkness at noon,
A sun-blazing night.

Has there been a native place
Found ever sweet?
Like a departure
It becomes a fire dream ready to rot.
Putting desperate pressure

On the burnt-out eyes
Man tracks down his own burning scar.
Let those willing to leave, be gone.
Yet who ever can endure
The whirling fire of nothingness?
Once drawn into it,
Who can get out, unscathed,
Unless he turns into a falling firebird,
Unless he turns into a falling meteorite?

HONG, Yunsuk (1925-   ). A native of Chongju, North Korea, Hong attended Teacher's College, Seoul National University. A member of the Korean Academy of Arts, she has published **Poems on the Koryo Dynasty** (1962), **A Wind Mill** (1963), **On Ornament** (1963), **Daily Clock Sound** (1971), **Sunlight of an Alien** (1974), **Women's Park** and **How to Live** (1983).

On Ornament

That a woman
begins to wear her ornaments
one after another
means she begins to shed her dreams
one after another.

A wistful desire
with which to shield with fingertips
the specks
where petals used to be.

Like Eve who covered
her shame with fig leaves
woman must make up with ornaments
for the loss of blossoms.

Do any teenagers wear
on their supple fingers
one-carat diamond rings?
They are dream itself.

Where love is gone,
where friendship and little start-dust dream
go rusty like a summer lawn,
autumn blows down a leaf.

To add ornament is
to call for nostalgia,
to grace the last season of the year.

To open the window through which
to learn the unpolluted loneliness
from the emerald blue,

Or it is just the ego that will not be lost,
or a wing on which are borne
the intent dreams of a woman.

Spring Fever

I am sick
gasping for breath,
at a touch of wind or a whiff of flower scent
Spring is like a wanton wife
giggling over the forsythia hedge

Hair let loose
hair shampooed glossy
It dazzles like a young wife
who grows daily mature and desirable

Chained to bed the man gets thirsty
His carefree wife hiding
behind the forsythia hedge
snickers for a whole day
and he turns yellow like jaundiced eyes
as he watches the yellow hedge

KIM, Jonggil(1926-). A native of Andong, North Kyongsang province Kim studied English at Korea University, where he teaches. In 1969 he went to Sheffield University in England where he met William Empson. Awardee of the Mogwol literature prize and an outstanding critic, he has published **Christmas** (1969), **At Hahwe** (1979) and **Heaven, Earth, Drought, Yellow** (1991).

Christmas

Like our hearts too hardened for tears
the skies promise no snow.

I stop in the darkening street
to search for the star in the east.

Bethlehem is far out of reach
though the same day comes every year.

Is it braying of a way-worn mule
that I hear faintly ringing in my ears?

I have no gold, nor myrrh, nor
frankincense in my briefcase, though.

Seized by wanderlust, I wish to roam
far into the cold for a sign of the birth.

Would I care at all if my Mary
were clad in simple dusty cotton?

A lantern-lit shack or a dingy waiting room
is more civilized than the straw-littered stable.

This is an idle thought, I know.
But just in return for what I feel for the night
May downy snowflakes fall to keep us warm;
My kindly snow falls like white blossoms.

Tavern at Sunset

The blazing sun gets cooled
at twilight like heated iron.

Rain drips somewhere in the corner
of my desolate youth
against the sunset of my life.

My lips burning red like a coxcomb
I down glass after glass of ice-cold rice wine.

Should all that my youth prizes and seeks
end in a mere glass of wine,

what else would I cling to,
fret about and regret?

Shouting my own name repeatedly
I fling myself onto the street
into the invading darkness.

KIM, Namjo (1927-). Born in Taegu, South Kyongsang province, Kim started writing while in college. It was not until the early fifties that she won due recognition. Currently she is teaching at Sungmyong Women's University. Among her books are **Life** (1952), **Tree and Wind** (1958) **A Flag in the Heart** (1959), **Music from the Maple Grove** (1963), **The Winter Sea** (1967), **Snowy Day** (1970), **Love in Grass Characters** (1974), **Accompanying** (1976), and **For the Poor Name** (1991).

The Winter Sea

I went out to the winter sea.
The strange birds
and my lovely ones
were dead and gone.

I was thinking of you
when the wind savagely howled
enough to freeze the truthful oath made in tears.

Fire of futility
was aflame on the swells of waves.

Not long
before I end my journey
with my prayer over;
let me invite a soul
that will open into a gate
for more passionate prayer.

Though not long
before I end my journey
I went out to the winter sea.
The waters of endurance
raised a pillar from the deep.

Music

Drowned in the perilous sea of music
I weep under its withering spell.

All my life
The eternal cloud drifting in my sky
has been soaked in sorrow.

I have yielded much poetry
yet not a piece has ever
worked out my salvation.

Man lives half his life
consuming it in chaotic scepticism
the other half is led
vulnerable to wounds.

Like trees that bristle in harmony
in the snow-piling woods,
like the night of peace
settling after sunset
I wish my life to be.

Truth is fear;
Falsity, disgrace.

I cry intoxicated with withering music
because it is truth, nothing else.

Heart's Flag

My heart is a flag
that is hoisted unnoticed
in time and space invisible.

When gripped by madding fever
I light out onto the crossroad
that thickens with snow
the flag's quiet shadow
veils the snow path as in smoke.

Is my heart's flag
listening to the music of snow?

I only wish each sunset
would go without regrets
that heap one after another like petals.

Could there be a gold-hearted friend
like the stretch of silken sands
where grief grave as an imperial edict has sunk?

My heart is a flag.
Sobbing quietly it prays
in time and space invisible.

MOON, Toksu (1927-) Born in Hamhan, South Kyongsang province, Moon was educated both at Hong-ik University and Korea University, where he majored in Korean. Though his earlier poems came out in 1947, his recognition came with his poems being published in **Hyondae Munhak** (Modern Literature) in 1956. Currently, Chairman of P.E.N., Korean Center, Moon attempts to employ a surrealistic technique in his writing. Among his works are **Ecstasy** (1956), **Line & Space** (1966), **Domicile** (1968), **Eternal Flower-garden** (1976) in collaboration with other, **June for the Survived** (1982), **Spanning a Bridge** (1982), **Selected Poems** (1983) and **For Those Thing That Fade** (1991).

Ode to Fallen Leaves

A leaf unhooked from the branch
descends gropingly as if to scratch the air,
a pain of parting from attachment.

In a rehearsing gesture
of all the earthly trials:
tumbling into a ravine,
sleighing down a hillslope,
rolling across a plain.

A leaf unhooked from the branch
comes to a halt, breathless,
on the cold asphalt pavement
in a posture of listening
for an on-coming footstep and its death.

A dead leaf intrudes, moth-soft,
into the room through a gaped window;
then descends unendingly
into a love one's soul
in a gesture of replanting the springtime.

Song for Grass Leaf

I have no wish at all other than
to grow as a tender grass blade
in the corner of a flower-bed in your heart
so that I may whisper forever
on the edge of your breath;
glisten in the dew of gathering tears
at a signal of your eyes

and fade away unnoticed on a late autumn day.
I have no wish at all
for I am a mere whiff of wind
that wanders in the woods of pre-existence,
a seed left unplanted in your heart.

Signpost

A piece of straw set adrift
is caught on a sign post
at the bottom of dead shallows
and is gifted with a breath of life.

As it tears the air quick as lightning
an angel's raiment is ripped on the edge;
it flutters like a flag
only to change into a bird
that soars into the skies.

Is it a signal sent down from God far away
on this particular night?

Threads of light
caught on a sign post
flutters like a golden butterfly
the size of heaven.

CHON, Pong-gon (1928-1988). Born in Anju, South P'yong-an province, North Korea, Chon came to the south shortly after the liberation of the country. His recognition came with his first poems being published in **Munye** (Literary Arts). He attempts to fuse lyricism with intellectual texture in his poems. His works include **War, Music and Hope** (1957), in collaboration with two others, **Repetition of Love** (1959), **In Search of Poetry** (1962), **Ch'unhyang's Love Song** (1967) and **The Inner Sea** (1970).

Mischief

I aim at a tree with a rifle.
I aim at a leaf on a tree-top.
Bored by the job
I suddenly tilt the muzzle up into the air
With the breech rubbing against my cheek.
The sky comes within the range of gunsight.
The sky grows big in the sight of an M.I.
I stand under the sky.
I look at the sky.
The small sky hurts my eyes.
The gunsight goes dim.
I quit my game.

The Piano

From the fingertips of a lady
sitting down at the piano
bounce
the live fish
unendingly
in tens
or
in twenties
on the tail
of flipping light.

I go out to the sea
to fetch in excitement
a sharpened knife blade
of the waves.

KIM, Kwangnim (1929-) Born in Wonsan, North Hamgyong province, North Korea, Kim began writing in his own words a semblance of poems in 1947. He was editor of **Modern Poetics and Vowels**. He attaches importance to employing imagery as an essence of a poem. He has published **Wounded Graft** (1959), **Bright Shadow of Imagery** (1962), **Casting a Net in the Morning** (1965), **The Fall of a Crane** (1971), **Twisted Vines** (1973), **A Mid-winter Walk** (1976), **Heavenly Flower** (1985), and **Flower-scent for an Upturned Nose** (1991).

The Lord's Day

A brood of fledgling swallows
was craving for food in yellow chorus;
the choir boys glisten like leaves
on an olive tree that tilts skyward.

The pipe organ grew parched
with thirst and I stepped down
on its glittering scales
toward a shaded monastery

which some altar boys, red bands
worn around their necks,
would visit three times a day
candlestick in hand;

They will shed light in heaven.

Conflict

I take for a change
my wife who has been driven into a quagmire of debt;
we get onto a deluxe highway bus
heading for a watering place.

For the first time
in eighteen years I watch her closely;
how thin she looks!
All these years
she has been hanging our children
on her twisted vines
like a cluster of wisteria blossoms,
for that is what she is — so skinny.

Her hands and feet have twisted so much
like vines around her heart that gets more entangled
against its wish to be freed apart.

How could our ties have been!

Look up in the skies
lest your labor be lost.

Why did you come into the world?
"To pay back my debts."

CH'ON, Sangbyong (1930-1993). Born in Ch'ang-won, South Kyongsang province, Ch'on left Seoul National University without a degree. His first poems appeared in **Munye** (Literary Arts) in 1952. His poems are characterized by childlike purity and innocence, bereft of technical trappings. He has published **Bird** (1971), **At Tavern** (1972), **Ch'on Sangbyong is a Born Poet** (1973) and **The Day When a Rambling on This Beautiful Earth Ends** (1991), selected poems.

Return to Heaven

I shall return to heaven
hand in hand with the dew
that evaporates in the dawning light.

I shall return to heaven
in company with the sunset-glow
when clouds beckon while I stroll on the shore.

I shall return to heaven
on a day when my beautiful earthly journey ends.
In heaven I will say every thing was so lovely on earth.

Namelessness

The sunset-glow so beautiful
beyond expression
was about to vanish

In the presence of the moment
and the oncoming night
I was thinking of tomorrow

Spring has gone.
Yesterday and this very moment
are burning — O the sunset-glow about to fade!

Why I have to cut a slice of blue
from the far-off sky and to etch
my namelessness without a day's delay

I wish to know,
I wish to know.

SHIN, Tong-yop (1930-1969). Born in Puyo, South Ch'ungchong province, Shin studied history at Konkuk University and majored in Korean literature while in graduate school. In 1956 he established himself as a poet with his prize-winning piece "*The Earth of a Plowman Who Talks*" coming out in a newspaper. His books are **Women of Asia** (1963), **The River Kum**, an epic, **Selected Poems**, posthumously published, and **Be Gone Husks** (1991) selected poems.

The Land of Flowering Azaleas

Flowering azaleas dotting
the roadside;
a common butterfly staying
poised on a rock's edge,
your rifle thrown down on the grass
you've gone to sleep,
I remember.

Where the rock lies, it's been said,
generals buried their comrades,
in the sun-bright days of old,
in the days of the late
Koguryo dynasty.

Those sick of waiting headed mountainward to death,
heaps of bones taking the mountainsides
by force like flowers in bloom.

You'd roll a cigarette and smile
a cheerless smile, saying your innocent
folks left behind in a village
far on the south sea
would go hungry, without food.

I've just seen somebody's ankle,
cut off, stuck in a boot
on a stony patch in the orchard.

All day long
bullets were raining
down the mountainsides.

Those sick of waiting headed mountainward to death.
On the flowering mountainsides
bullets were raining down all day.

Flowering azaleas dotting
the roadside;
A fair-looking youth lay
cold and dead
in the rock shade.

A fighter plane passed overhead
machine-gunning the flowering village
and was gone.

Those sick of waiting
headed mountainward to death,
their longing flared
up heaven, their bones
taking the mountainsides
by force.

Where the rock lies, it's been said,
generals buried their comrades,
in the days of the late
Koguryo dynasty,
in the days of warm wind blowing.

You lay bleeding,
your cigarette case
thrown down on the grass.

YI, Hyonggi (1933-   ). Born in Chinju, South Kyongsang province, Yi studied Buddhism at Tongguk University. His recognition as a poet came in 1949 while he was in high school. A fine critic as well as a poet, he teaches at his alma mater. His books are **The Bleak Country** (1973), **Poem of a Stone Pillow** (1973), **Drought in a Dream** (1977) and **Even Though the Star Flow like Water** (1991), selected poems.

Fallen Petals

It is graceful to see one
sensible enough to leave
when it is time to leave

Through the inferno
of springtime passion
my love is fading now

Petals showering down
we must leave now
loaded with bliss of parting

Into the deep of thick shade
into the autumn about to ripen with fruit
my youth fades like a flower.

Let us part
waving our pale hands
when petals start showering down to the ground

Farewell, my beloved,
you're my soul's sad eyes that deepen
like water filling up a well-spring

Song of Cricket

A cricket ripples sorrow
in the autumn night
like a running brook.

On the thatched roof,
on the paper-torn sliding door,
on the eyelids of one quietly asleep,
an old tale slumbers
with time coiled like growth rings,

The bright moon
prompts my tears.

This autumn night
all that has passed and gone
comes back to life, remembered
and a cricket releases a song,

Oh, a piece of masterpiece.

PARK, Hijin (1931-). Born in Yonchon, Kyonggi province, Park graduated from Korea University where he majored in English. A series of poems including "*Ode to Merciful Bodhisattv*a" which was published in 1956 established him as a talented poet. Among his works are **Chamber Music** (1960), **The Bronze Age** (1965), **Smiling Silence** (1970), **Between Light and Darkness** (1976), **314 Quatrains** (1982), **A Dream in Iowa** (1985), **Poet, Be a Prophet** (1985), **Lovers among Lilacs** (1985) and **A Drop of Encounter** (1991).

Ode to Merciful Bodhisattva

Standing aloft on lotus blossoms
that will stay forever unfaded,
for they are carved in stone,
thou reignest timeless
over the finite of this world,
so close to us
yet at a far distance.

What waves in the ocean
can ever roll in to wash
the edge of thy feet?
What winds of the world
can ever rustle
against thy ethereal garment?

Thine eyes half closed
are forever about to open, so bright;
thy smile faintly playing on thy closed lips
will never fade
for it is part of eternity.
Thy mind shining like the sun,
thy person shining like the sun,
thy person suffused with flower scent,
thou quietly listenest in that mirror
held up to thine ever-shining spirit
to the procession of myriad stars.

Thou holdest in thy hand
a dream-held string of beads,
no finger stirring a breath of life.
Thy presence strikes me speechless;
thy beauty drives us to despair.
And like a creature waiting calmly

for his death
I have only drawn sighs.

Merciful Bodhisattva!

When I regard you from this distance
I can hardly think about the touch
of a supreme artist
but I have only one wish to make in earnest,
though it may sound foolish;
May I write one single poem
to remember thee by,
the most beautiful poem ever written,
so that each word and phrase
may illuminate thy consummate virtue.
I wish to write such a poem
too exquisite to call my own.

Song for Empty Cup

A woman living single
has sent a man living single
a wine cup of simple white porcelain.

The man, his hands washed clean,
sat down quietly;
He was reaching his hand
to touch its smooth skin

when the air filling up
the empty wine cup
dissolved of itself
into sweet wine.
Belatedly the man realized with a nod
that it was no empty cup
that she had sent him.

KWON, Ilsong (1933-). Born in Sunchang, North Cholla province, Kwon went to Chonnam National University, where he studied engineering. He came to establish himself as a poet with his prize-winning piece *"Sleepless" Badge* coming out in a newspaper in 1957. His books are **This Land Makes Me Drink** (1966), **Slash and Burn People in the City** (1969), **The Woman of the Sea** (1982), **Between Wind and Tears** (1987), **Bibichu's Love** (1988) and **Tango on the Sea** (1991).

The Apocalypse

At 7 p.m. in a saloon downtown Seoul
when a bottle of gin is finished
night gyrates to cast a spell
over us, her and me.

At the base of a cliff
where one day's summarized career
lies limp, water-wet,
my eager hand edges its way
along the Monte Carlo beach
till it shuttles in and out of her womb.

I hear her heart on fire.
Her burning frame, sharp in her appetite,
wriggles, serpent-like,
gripping my limbs as in a vise,
when a start signal
launches our capacity loaded ship.

What fun, my Eve!
I kiss repeatedly
to commemorate my occupation
of your citadel.
Who can blame what we are up to?

An apple glows red, bestial
by my bedside;
I float in midair,
my dangling neck suspended in the void.

Rapture

Breaking into a baby's breath,
she's stepped out her hard shell,
bereft of her wild roaring instinct;
she turns her back on a heavy
sheeting of rain-storms
that rip heaven and earth apart.

The most gorgeous jewel is brought
into my soul at this hour
when she strokes with her pure
and unstained hands
the empty space where a white horse
soars beating his wings.

Now turned
to misty rain
she cries silently
the way the gentle breeze
stirs a susurrus in the pine grove.

PARK, Chaesam (1933-). Born in Tokyo, Japan, Park left Korea University without a degree. He established himself as a promising young poet with his poems first coming out in **Hyondae Munhak** (Modern Literature) in 1955. His peculiar lyric style is in the tradition of Korean poetry. His works include **Ch'unhyang's Mind** (1961), **In the Sunlight** (1970), **A Thousand Year-old Wind** (1975), and **Autumn River Where Weeping Burns** (1991).

A Landscape

As the wind scuds across the green grass
so the sun ricochets on the southern seas.

Soon a seagull or two whirls
over the sailboats
that drift in flashes into dots
as if bound for a distant shore.

My heart aches to see
those sails gleaming white;
how far will they go before
turning back, tired?

Is the wind looking for shelter
in the shade of flowers
that are about to fade?
Is the sun seeking shelter in the wings
of those birds or under those gleaming sails?

Tell me, friends,
where this world and the next
part company.

As the wind scuds across the green grass
so the sun ricochets on the southern seas.

Flute Holes

The sunshine, it seems,
amuses itself most
with leaves and waters.
So does the moonshine, it seems,
in this care-worn world.
Should I claim remotest kinship to them?
Torn between parental solicitude and brotherly service;
molded into a stained pattern;
turned into flute holes etched in my own flesh
I weep like a submerged tree,
I weep like a waded-in water.

HONG, Yun-gi (1933-). Born in Seoul, Hong went to Hankuk University of Foreign Studies, where he studied English. He established himself as a poet with his first poems being published in **Hyondae Munhak** (Modern Literature) in 1959. In the same year he won a prize in the poetry contest sponsored by a newspaper. Working for the Korean Broadcasting System, he stays in Japan as a research fellow at Senshu University (1991-1992), Japan. His works include **My First Encounter with the Sea** (1986), **A Humble Flower** (1986), and **A Letter from a Poet** (1991).

Thunder

In the night after the azalea
festival on Mount Chiri
everybody had dropped to sleep
beaten up by fatigue
before sheets of sudden rain
and crazy crashes of thunder
shook me awake; I sat up, scared.

The mountain deity
that keeps all the peaks under his thumb
must be venting his wrath, it seems,
flagellating the earth with a vengeance.

My guess was that he's
storming us to repent of our sins
that blacken our souls.

Maple Leaves

In high spirits a gang
of ruddy-faced cheeks keep shouting
as they scale the cliffside

Forceful in their vocal bands
they continue shouting
setting the whole mountains on fire

which are devoured by flame
burning red-hot
like a volcanic eruption

Caught in fire
trapped in burning mountains
I should and shout in company.

PARK, Song-yong (1934-). A native of Haenam, South Cholla province, Park graduated from Chungang University, where he studied Korean. In the words of Park, Namsu, he belongs in the main tradition of Korean lyric poetry, coated with a touch of modernistic technique. Awarded several literary prizes, he has published **Things Lost in Autumn** (1969), **Spring, Summer, Autumn & Winter** (1970), **Winter Camellia in Bloom** (1977), **A Whistling Bird** (1982), **Flower-adorned Bier** (1987) and **Homeland On the Ends of the Earth** (1991).

The Opium Poppy *

Ready to faint when held;
to crumble when hugged,
that flower is no other than the opium
poppy whose fume once drowsed
the whole of China.
Just a frail annual plant,
it flares up my sunset garden
with its charm and beauty.

Eyes closed
I see Emperor Shien of T'ang dynasty,
King Sou dance a made dance
and Yangguefei dance
in the sleek nude..

Ready to snap when shaken,
more enchanting when pressed by lips,
the voluptuous beauty
of that poppy, a mere yearly plant,
once drowsed the whole of China.

Eyes closed,
I see them dance,
a throng of beauties in the nude
dance around the poppy;
dance drunk with dance.

* Named after yangguefei, the flower refers to the episode of her reigning beauty which captivated Emperor Shien of the Middle Kingdom and finally brought the empire and the ruler to ruin.

Fruit Tree

Can anything surprise me more
than the fruit maturing on a tree?

Taking root in barren red soil
its boughs beaten by weather
the fruit tree chooses autumn
when things start to fall
for the glory of colors and a load of grace.

Can anything surprise me more
than the fruit maturing on a tree?

I drift the whole year away,
going over a poem or two once in a while.
Come autumn I recover my vision
at the miracle of the fruit tree.

PARK, Pong-u (1934-1990). Born in Kwangju, South Cholla province, Park graduated from Chonnam National University, where he majored in Political Science. His recognition came with his prize-winning piece "The Truce Line" coming out in a newspaper in 1956. He was awarded a couple of literary prizes. His works include **The Truce Line** (1957), **A Flower-tree That Blooms in Winter** (1959), **A Grass Leaf in the Wasteland** (1976) and **Butterfly and Barbed Entanglements** (1991), selected poems posthumously published.

The True Line *

* The Military demarcation line dividing Korea into north and south.

Mountains face each other; distrusting eyes look at each other
with a glare. Aware that the volcano will explode any day like
a thunderbolt from the dark, should we remain feckless as frail
flowers?

The chill landscapes stare upon each other. Shall we hear no more
in this sweet land the brave mind sung of our ancestors and
the heroic legends of ancient kingdoms? The stars above can happily
share the same old skies; only we are torn apart, unable
to shed the slough of suffering, the gnawings of agony.

Blood has ceased to bathe the country; we stand here where
no single tree is safe to grow. Our old wounds still hurt us;
are we having a short recess or plying with empty talks?

O viper-tongue wind full of hate, will you bring us to bear
the rigors of another winter? How long can these frail flowers
endure living out their lives. Is this the only fair choice
left to us to make?

Mountains face each other; distrusting eyes look at each other
with a glare. Aware that this volcano will explode any day
like a thunderbolt from the dark, should we remain feckless
as frail flowers?

KIM, Yangshik (1931-) Born in Seoul, Kim graduated from Ehwa Women's University, where she studied English. She continued to study at graduate school, Tongguk University, majoring in Indian literature and Indian philosophy. Currently she heads Korean Association of Indian Literature. She has published **The Song of Chongup** (1969), **Collected Poems** (1974), **A Tomcat** (1980) and **Sparrows at Socho-dong** (1990).

Grass Flower

The days of old
the lonely days that have passed
now waver, my eyes closed

Each of us shall
be a grass flower
or a grass leaf

Again I shall die
only to be another grass flower
or grass leaf breathless in grief

I shall lie down on the grass leaf
to pluck a grass flower

I remember those innocent days of old
that waver, my eyes closed

Come tenderness so gentle
and I will let you go with a kiss

The grass flower
invades my heart
in waves of sorrow

I tiptoe skyward
to hug the scented wind, whirling
I shall perish only to be a grass leaf

On the grass leaf I lie down
to pluck a grass flower

Elegy

Because of you I have lived
Because of your call I have lived
O my love
O my love

My voiceless shouting
that stabs the sky
no more reaches you now
but condenses into snow
piling on the peaks far out
drifting back into the ancient times

KIM, Yojong (1933-). Born in Chinju, South Kyongsang province, Kim graduated from Sunggyungwan University, where she studied Korean. Her recognition came in 1968 when her poems first came out in **Hyondae Munhak** (Modern Literature). She has three books of poems to her credit: **Harmony** (1969), **Sunlight Descending on the Sea** (1973) and **The Sea of Lemon** (1976).

Labyrinth

My niece past marriageable age
and I much older
strolled arm in arm
on Chongno street
in early summer morning
brighter than crystal clear
and we pushed open a door
of an exclusive jeweller's
to get side by side
into the turquoise of heaven

Browsing through the garden
overgrown with ruby
next to the mossed woods of emerald
my niece past marriageable age
lost herself into a one-karat diamond
while I was circling inside a pair
of pure gold rings
in search of her, lost and gone,
when I caught sight of moon and stars and dew
and found her turned to moon, to star
or dew until she came out blinded
in many years of being locked inside
a piece of jewel
at the brilliant rays of sun
on the summit of Mont Blanc
only to fall into Lake Leman

where she was coral-swaying
before she was hauled out
from Helio's gold net
and fell asleep lying on the sands
as she was spinning a dream of opal
with waves rolling in and out
over the white soles of her feet.

By the time Alexandrian port wine
grew mature in the hollow navel
of my niece soaked in the waves
I came, bedeviled by flame and flood,
from the world beyond
until she came to
her eyes opening brightly
like gardenia in the moonlight.

The Sea of Lemon

From flower that captivates me
from love that captivates me
from God who controls me
from lemon smell that grips me
I wish to be released
I wish to bleed in released agony

To bleeding enemy
to bleeding angel
to bleeding lemon meat
I wish to give a kiss
I wish to tremble to loneliness that kiss

Wounded lemon
in the bleeding sea
I wish to salvage the thick summer foliage
in the wake of a martyred death

KO, Un (1933-). A native of Kunsan, North Cholla province, Ko was forced to discontinue his formal education while in middle school due to the Korean war. In 1952 he became a Buddhist monk and led a life of meditation for 10 years before returning to secular life. His first poems came out in 1958. One of the strong dissident voices, Ko heads the Federation of Writers for National Literature. Among his books are **Entering Nirvana** (1960), **Verse Collection for the Seashore** (1964), **O Senoya** (1970), **In the Village of Munhi** (1977), **Road at dawn** (1978), **The Star of My Country** (1984), **Poem, Fly Away** (1986), **Your Eyes** (1988), and **The Morning Dew** (1990).

The Sky

Listen,
how man has murdered the earth;
how he is poisoning the ocean
till he has nothing left
but the sky.
How long can he endure
the skies?

O blue sky that will die
and my own death in its wake!

Chongno Street *

* One of the busiest streets in Seoul

I stop on the way
standing for a good while
and watch every one that passes
carrying a purchase of grief-load.
Destroy realities, destroy realities.

I stop on the way
standing for a good while.
Listen, all grief-laden creatures.
Let my heart be daubed
in potassium cyanide
to burn down everything that has
been grieving these twenty years,
these thirty years long.

For a good while
I stop on the way.
All have gone,
doors slamming each to each,
neonlights turned off.
Let my bald head beat against the curfew bell,
butting it with the crown of head.

The whole city lying asleep,
watch me scatter the white of my brain
under the booming of the bell
till it echoes as far as the Western sea.

KIM, Huran (1934-). Born in Seoul, Kim attended the Teachers College of Seoul National University. Her recognition came in 1961 when her poems began to appear in major literary magazines. Her poems are mostly simple vignettes of ordinary life and nature and compact in tactile imagery. She has published **Ornamental Knife and Rose** (1959), **Musical Scale** (1971), **Certain Waves and Collected Poems** (1985).

Winter Tree

The tree keeps silence,
eyes clammed shut,
lost in deep thought.

As if to flash back light
I turn into a tree,
tossing silence in response.

The wind rises.
The cold moon passes a wakeful night
in mossed silence.

When no one anticipates the arrival of spring
the tree tells me what it is like
to wait in patience.
The spring is nesting in my breast.

Fish Cooking

The sea has invaded the kitchen.
The waves surge on a chopping board.

To remove its coat of mail
that challenges the sun and
to chop it into several cuts
take a certain measure of courage.

The world has already gone eye-shut.
Against the staircase
that slopes seaward
the waves foam sprawling,
knife blade held between their teeth.

KIM, Jaihiun (1934-). Born in Kwangju, South Cholla province, Kim studied English both at Hankuk University of Foreign Studies and University of Massachusetts, U.S.A., where he earned two graduate degrees. He taught English and creative writing in an American college before returning home to Korea in 1971. His poems in English started to be published in 1960s in the States. His poems in Korean came out in 1975. His books include 10 volumes, five of them in English: **Detour** (1972), **A Pigsty Happiness** (1973), **Dawning and Home-thought** (1976), **Nature Man** (1988); the rest in Korean: **Revolt of Soil** (1975), **Drifting Life** (1979), **Dancing Weeds** (1982), **A Certain Hug** (1986) and **Rainbow in the City** (1990). Kim has so far translated more than 2300 Korean poems into English.

The Law of Fall

The mist enfolding the mountainsides
condenses into dewdrops;
the rocks loaded with the weight of millennial years
begin to crumble in running sand-grains.

A young bonze, canonized as a high priest,
sees his earthly existence end,
his own frame blazing on a pyre.

In the far-away valley of life
past years all seem but yesterday.

The red-flaming apples
and the larks soaring into the blue heaven
are destined to drop to the ground
with the arrival of nightfall;
the snowflakes swirling in a frolic
settles quietly toward twilight.

Like a meteorite stuck cold in earth
after having shot splendidly across the sky
all struggles and strife
submit to the law of fall.

To a Nigerian Friend

Material voluptuousness vexed you.
You saw through the emptiness of luxury.
Progress wasn't equal to comfort.
Stranded by choice on the soil to which
your ancestors had been sold as slaves
you commanded respect and due pride for
what your African heritage stood for.
You offered me what you were,
not what you had; and I was happy
to return your gift in kind.
We must have been of one blood and flesh
in a former life or we are part
of the Master Spirit in man.

Mother-thought

Your face,
geography of sorrows,
wrecked by headwinds
through the harshness of time,
turned into a plaster image.

Gentleness in your eyes
reminding me of Bodhisattva
ripples into my memory,
generosity radiating.

Yours was a simple wish:
to visit a famed temple.
What if they ask me about it, you said,
once across the eternal river?

Foolishness of your son
to mock your simplicity.
Caught in the whirligig of human concerns,
free-wheeling for years,
grasping void after void,
you turned into a plaster image.

Your face,
geography of sorrows.

SHIN, Kyongnim (1936-) Born in Chungwon, North Ch'ungchong province. Shin studied English at Tongguk University. His first poems appeared in **Munhak Yesul** (Literary Arts) in 1956. His poems in general concern misery, anger, regrets, and bitterness of the farming population. His works include **Farmers' Dance** (1973), **The Ridge** (1979) and **Summer's Day** (1991), selected poems.

Visiting a Rural Town

A market day it was, more deserted
than any other day;
the droughts had dried up paddy fields enough to raise dust;
roofs and stone walls look languished as farmers.

Our bus stopped at a general store
from which I could see my wife's grave in the distance.
I brought my son along into a roadside stand
where we drank tepid soft drinks
manufactured with foreign capital.

Meeting with my friends I hadn't long seen
I wondered why their eyes were shot with blood.
Mute and silent,
they just shook my hand,
forced smiles painted on their faces.

The chicken-house alley was littered
with stone, sticks and hoes.
I remember that place from across the barber's;
there farmers and coal miners would shout
curses at grips in a fight;
a sidewalk lined with rice dealers;
the volunteer fire fighters
who would scramble down the alley.

A market day it was, more deserted
than any other day.
Callused hands held my hand tight
as if reluctant to let me go
the day I came to visit my wife's grave.

Reed

The reed had been weeping
silently and inwardly
since when, no one knows
until one night, of a sudden,
it came to realize
that its whole frame was swaying.

It wasn't the wind nor moonlight
but his own weeping
that caused his shaking,
yet he knew nothing about it.

To live is to weep
silently and inwardly,
it did not notice it before.

KIM, Yongtae (1936-). Born in Seoul, Kim went to Hong-ik University, where he majored in fine arts. His recognition came with ''Snow Scene'' being published in a magazine in 1959. His poems tend to explore the psychological region of human situations. His books are **The Village of the Jews** (1965), **Mean Ratio** (1968) in collaboration with others, **Cigarettes for the Guests** (1978), and **Autumn, Weight of Melody** (1991).

Hotel North

A couple of angels get in,
the door closed behind them.
Made of paper, neither of them
can pull at the other
nor knock the other down.
The building itself is of paper;
a single step
will send it crumbling flat.
The water in the paper vase
as blue as blue can be.
As it's fresh from the spring
there's no use worrying
if the flowers in the vase will fade.
The only thing that is alive
is the water that ripples
or the flower that drops
its beautiful petals, one by one.

Landscape I

A lake comes in view
A swan floats in it
Fairly good
Boughs of trees are mirrored in the water
I often tremble
despite my firm hold on the heart
I cannot help it
The swan floats around a corner
The currents lie in a slumber
All goes fairly well
And yet I am all alone
all in a tremble
I immediately notice a sign
that something has sunk or
gone crumbling in my heart

HWANG, Tong-gyu (1938-). Born in Seoul, Hwang studied English literature at Seoul National University, where he presently teaches. He went to Edinburg University for a year's research. His poems in general are an attempt to seek his identity in the vortex of maddening realities. His works include **One Fine Day** (1961), **Rain Falling in the South** (1975), **When I see a Wheel I Like to Roll It** (1978), **Wind Burial** (1984), and **Who Is Afraid of Alligators** (1986).

A Small Love Song

Your letter came with our yesterdays tied to it.
The paths I had followed you on all these years
have suddenly vanished.
Many other things have also gone out of sight.
The pebbles we used to play with as children
have scattered, embedded in the earth, hidden from view.
I love you, I love you, and in the cold evening sky
I see gold slowly beaten into a glittering dome.
Light snow starts swirling
in thin flakes,
unprepared to land upon the earth.
A few flakes float forever in the air,
stricken by insomnia.

A Smaller Love Song

A few scraps of the wind
that has not ceased to blow
The wet snow that falls
at supper-time or a waterdrop
that keeps running
dissolves in midair before falling
A waterdrop brushes you by
drawn from one wind to another
as you suddenly spread your arms

CHONG, Hyon-jong (1939-   ) Born in Seoul, Chong graduated from Yonsei University, where he studied philosophy. He had been affiliated with journalism as a reporter before he took up teaching at Seoul Junior College for Arts. His first poems were published in **Hyondae Munhak** (Modern Literature) in 1965. His books are **The Dream of Things** (1972), **Festivity of Suffering** (1974), and **I Am Uncle Star** (1978), and **There Is an Island between People** (1991).

Note 25

When a person cannot dispense with something
we say he is addicted to it. A dope fiend, for
instance, cannot go a single day without drug
None of us, however, who cannot go without food,
are said to be food-addicts. I for one feel myself
addicted to food, for I can hardly stand a single
day on empty stomach and so I must be a food-addict.
Narcoticism is an offense against the law while
food-addiction is considered a lawful act duly
sanctioned by society. That is, a victory of one
form of addiction over another. Man's life, in fact,
is addicted to struggle, a victory-addiction.
In a hustle I wake up early today to go gloriously
to work so that I may hunt for daily bread, for I am
a food-addict. Drunk with feeding myself, I am an
unmistakable addict.

Miserable

When I've finished a poem
I should bury it in the ground
or in the heaven.
Why should I be in a hurry to publish it?
Miserable me, O!
No matter how I try to hide myself
my shabbiness shows.

Going by far

Shall we go to the sea
and become a blowing sea wind
or to a very cold climate
and turn to falling snow
or head to a warm territory
and be shining rays of sunlight
or go far west where the sunset
blazes red, melting in the evening glow?
This is how life shows in its greatest beauty.

YI, Kunbae (1940-) Born in Tangjin, South Ch'ungchong province, Yi graduated from Sorabol Arts College, where he studied creative writing. Considered one of the promising young talents, he has won many literary awards. He also shows a finesse in sijo, traditional verse form. He has published **Flower-tree That Plays a Love-song** (1960), **O Song** (1981), and **What the Stone Turtle Says in the East Sea** (1982).

The Winter Vision

With vision out of the reach of the field edges
I watch the open space
where a mountain springs into being and perishes
and something made impossible to be alive
advances toward me,
a mass of sunlight,
a greenstuff tasselled with leaves;
the mountain incarnate approaches my door
shaking snow off.
When I meet you, my throat clear,
nothing is visible in the field;
yet I watch the open space in the field.

A Certain Year

"Alas! You have flown away like a wild bird." - Chiyong -

There's something that does not return, once gone
Can a slice of rotten fruit meat turn
to earth, to water or to wind?
Nature wails while calling
for something that will not return
Let me call back the evening-tide of the village
where things mortal delight in living
The remaining life-span of a wild flower
that has sustained in obscurity
flares up in a roaring sound
somewhere on the cold winter sky

A shaft of light filters through a papered window
Spoons clinking, laughters ruffling
Mother grows to be grandmother
Graves alone remain
Snow falls

SONG, Sugwon (1940-). Born in Kohung, South Cholla province, Song went to Sorabol Arts College, where he received training in creative writing. His recognition came in 1975 when he won the New Poet Prize from Munhak Sasang (Literature and Thought), and again his epic "The Tonghak Uprising" won him the Prize of the Minister of Culture and Information. He has seven books of poems to his credit: **Against the Temple Gate** (1980), **A Dreaming Island** (1982), **The Dumb Jar** (1984), **O Bird, Blue Bird** (1986), **Out Land** (1988), **I Smile While Asleep When I Think of You** (1991) and **Guarding the Starry Night** (1992).

The Cuckoo on Mt. Chiri *

* The name of a mountain some 6,300 feet high bordering the three southern provinces; South Cholla, South Kyongsang, and North Cholla.

Many a cuckoo on many a mountain peak
was carolling in unison
'cuckoo', 'cuckoo'.
It wasn't until thrice three springs
passed, leaving me seasoned with sorrow,
that many a cuckoo turned out
to be a single bird.

A single cuckoo
hiding down the side of Mt. Chiri
uttered a cry,
which the next peak echoed
and again echoes the peak after the next
until it seemed many cuckoos were crying
in unison.

I saw that the chain of mountain peaks
was gradually settling in stillness
with the cuckoo's crying gone
when a silent river started to run.

I saw the Somjin River
rolling down in swelling waves
lap the shores of many an isle
that dots the southern sea.

I saw the cuckoo singing on a livelong spring day
down the side of Mt. Chini, as though drained of its tears
left of this world and remembered as the last sorrowful hues
in which the flaming azaleas glow on the pebbles.

Poem

Water wears away a rock
when rock cannot wear it.
Storms will fell a tree but
they can hardly hurt the roots.

This morning a Japanese cedar
has collapsed on the fleecy snow.

A small force moves our soul;
a thousand-mile flight of a wild goose
is possible with frail feathers.

KIM, Chi-ha (1941-). Born in Mokpo, a port city in South Cholla province, Kim studied Aesthetics at Seoul National University. In 1969 **Shi-in** (Poets) published his first poems. During the seventies and the early eighties he was imprisoned due to his political activism against the dictatorial rule. His "*Five Thieves*" is a poignant attack on those involved in corruption. His works include **Loess** (1970), **In Burning Thirst** (1981), **Great Narrative: South** (1982) and **Longing for the Last Piece of Flesh** (1991). He was awarded **Lotus Prize** in 1975 by Asian and African Writers and Poetry International in 1981.

Bird

The blue sky spreads over the fleecy
clouds and the glittering hills.
Bird on the wing,
why do you tear my chained heart
and make me sad?

Let me sink my teeth
in the deepest layer of my flesh;
the blood runs from a wound
from clawing the whole night
and decays on hot summer's days.

Break this earth-bound frame loose
just for once day or night.
My sad eyes and my blood-soaked body
wilt so weakened, unable to stand and struggle.
Bird, come listen to the clanging chains.

How long before I'll come to thee,
bird that flits across my soul's fields
where thin lights grow dimmed
against the bright rays of the day?

Now I see you flee off the blue sky-edge
beyond the blue mountains.
Why do you tear my chained heart
and make me sad?
Clouds fleet in an endless glitter.

Aerin I *

* Suggestive of an ideal, love, pity, hope, etc.

The bird cried only once
and fled away.
How its note wakes up my heart!
O the rising sun that flashes fulgently
for a brief moment before it fades!
How could I ever know
a glistening dew grips
me in joy!

If only once
for a single day
or only for an hour
I did not love you
with true love.
How could I know
that you'd sustain my existence
I could pin my hope on.

Aerin,
Both my eyes and hands pulled out and cut off,
both my limbs chopped off,
reduced to a dump of garbage
from which mindless red flesh shows.

Aerin!
Aerin!
I call you, Aerin.

Aerin 4

There was a time when I could
hardly bring myself to say
''I'm lonely.''
Now I should speak
in a loud voice
into the hollow of heaven
''I'm lonely.''

Gleams of light that sweep across my breast;
between those rays thin shafts
gleam in and out and pass
through the days that are gone.
The more they pass,
the thinner they become.
And it hurts me.

Though I have a big mouth for speech
there's no one alive on earth
I can talk to now.
Though I clench my fist
there's nothing any longer
to be held in my hand.

There's no trace of longing
left in this place; the night rain is falling
and a note wafting from the blind flautist
makes me this lonely.

YI, Songbu (1942-). Born in Kwangju, South Cholla province, Yi graduated from Kyunghee University, where he studied Korean. His first poems came out in **Hyondae Munhak** (Modern Literature) in 1962. He has published **Poems** (1969), **Our Food** (1974), **A Trip to the Paekcje Dynasty** (1974) and **Clean Country** (1991), selected poems.

Paddies

Paddies lean against each other
for survival.
The hotter the sun grows
the sooner they attain maturity;
out of self-love
each leaves its own self to its neighbor's care.

The nation grows stronger
when each part is bound to the whole.
We can imagine some minds boiling with fury
when charged guilty despite innocence.
When the paddies start dancing apart
from each other they are doomed to vanish silently.

Paddies know how to keep fit,
their sad eyes rinsed clean in the autumn sky;
they know how to hide their anger
in a breath of air.
They know their heart is warm.

The bounty of this love
given by the paddies as a parting gift,
this heart-felt longing left to us
as they fall and fall only to rise,
the bounty of this strength.

The Bulldozer

The mass of hill is rammed down at dawn.
One shoulder blade dislocated from each frame,
the bodies bleed, rammed down;
repeatedly rammed down until they are
heaped into another hill of challenge.
All night long
faces of men, their will-power suicided;
minds of men inured to inner anger

are rammed down to assault another hill;
a breath whiffs from where the hill has been razed,
energy wriggles alive while being chopped into bits.
Still warm enough,
still generous enough
it hates no one,
big chunks of its flesh ripped apart.
Regard the other mass of hill, its mighty weight
becoming a huge grave, far from being rammed down.
Listen to the word compelling love by death.

How could it be removed to another land?
How could tens of thousands of truckloads
of earth get rid of it?

KIM, Yon-gyun (1942-). Born in Kimje, North Cholla province, Kim studied creative writing at Sorabol Arts College. His recognition came in 1971 with a series of poems published in literary magazines. Currently working for a publishing house, he has published **Rainy Season** (1974), **The Seagull** (1977), **The Sea and Children** (1979) and **Man** (1983).

Years

Who knows?
A man fallen down in the furrow of time
turns to tears, an embittered spirit
that roams unable to reach the grave
over this world like shiftless
sleet that dampens the ditch.

Who knows?
We, swarming onto time's wind,
onto time's grassland,
will be gone
and scatter away
as when leaves drop with the arrival of autumn;
as when you, O Father, left me for good.

Years and months, as I watch you,
a grass flower opening at dawn
prompts my tears, my tears.

Message

- lament over the passing -

Time passes
We pass while kneeling down on the road
The unending flow of the mind for cherished things
passes and so love passes too
The budding wind that has knocked yesterday down,
the fiery wind that billows up and flees away
rises again
like a seed leaf sprouting in green.
Vanity vanity
All is vanity.
When I pass away on a far-off day
or my trace blooms into heat haze
remember how I have grieved while alive

over my eventual loss
how I have passed away
grieving over my own loss

Remember me. Remember me.

PARK, Chech'on (1945-). Born in Seoul, Park left Tongguk University without a degree. His recognition came with his first poems coming out in **Hyondae Munhak** (Modern Literature) in 1966. Winner of several literary prizes he has published **On Changtze** (1975), **Mind Law** (1979), **Rule** (1981), **The Third Star** (1983) and **Heavenly Flower** (1991). Currently he works for the Korean Arts and Culture Foundation.

Distrust

Better not to be born; to die is to suffer.
Do not quit life; to be born again is to suffer.
This is what Christ said.
Life and death alike are suffering,
our old masters said more briefly.
It is futile to tell life from death.
Who could leave his presence behind
and who else would regain it?
It is so ridiculous for mere grass
to remark about this or that.

Heavenly Traveler
     -Tu Fu-

What if I should go deaf and wakeful when, old, I quit drinking?
Then let me pick up a monkey's chattering in the wind.
I would stay awake overnight pondering over the leaves
    that fall far in the distance.
I would follow the sound of water that fades at a bend.
I would be flying as a heavenly traveler and
    think of the white hairs beneath my ears.
In the whirligig of life, I would die a wild goose's cold legs.

Changtzu 33

Every heavenly orbit is furrowed into a rose-garden.
My lifetime is draped in a robe of wind.
The way is open on karma's knife-edge
that strikes off rose-sprigs, coming and going.
O currents of my blood fleeing into the wind!
O rose-petals blown off by the wind!

KANG, Un-gyo (1945-). Born in Seoul, Kang studied English at Yonsei University. Her recognition came in 1968 with her prize-winning poem "A Pilgrim's Sleep" being published in **Sasanggye** (The World of Thoughts). She was awarded a writer's prize in 1975. She has published **Nothingness** (1971), **Grass Leaves** (1974), **A Diary of the Poor** (1977) and **You Are A Deep River** (1991).

Rotation (1)

The day draws to a close.
Far empty fields fall down.
Winds are folded in the savannah of sky;
man flutters all by himself.
Rows of houses in the street ripple.
The last ray of the sun is dragging
the city God knows where to.

The day draws to a close.
Day after day fair girls across the land
fall and pile up in heaps;
they are in a hurry while asleep,
grains of sands running ceaselessly
from off their beds.
Exposed to the light of many dark
centuries of life-and-death
no one can hide his own skin
that peels off one layer after another.

Houses start sobbing.
The day draws to a close.
A life-time swings, wind-locked,
like a falling fruit.
The ticking of the clock of the outspread skies
hangs secretly on every rooftop;
how the girls of sand
pile up in the wasteland!

We leave behind us
the longest shadow
as we fall apart.

Grass Leaves

I know a wind
that will blow in far-off days;
in far-off days snow and rain
Will peek through the window of a house.
Awake in the middle of night
I step out of my body
and see you leave in tears,
squeezing a yellow handkerchief,
wiping away in vain the ever-flowing blood;
just for a day or two
you will look up at the sunset before you leave.
We know all
even if we lie down twice on the ground.

HO, Hyongman (1945-). A native of Sunchon, South Cholla province, Ho graduated from Chonnam National University, where he studied Korean. His recognition came in 1973 when his first poems were published in **Wolgan Munhak** (Monthly Literature). He has four books of poems to his credit. **Clear Day** (1978), **Grass Leaves Say to God** (1984), **Lifting a Mosquito Net** (1985) and **Confuting the Inquisition** (1988). Currently he teaches at Mokpo University.

Snowfall on the Seas

You have gone, oh, my friend, leaving me
standing on the shore of Mokpo,
from which I watch the snow fall
thick and fast on the coastal seas
in a glitter like your departed spirit.
On the calm sea the snow
dissolves as it descends.
What song shall I sing for you
when I cannot so much whistle, vise-jawed, tongue-tied?
You have gone, oh, my friend, leaving me
all alone. No one can be free
from worldly cares and pains, I know.
I watch from this shore the snow
swirling in midair in a glitter
like your departed spirit,
falling thick and fast
on the coastal seas.

For the Poor

Frail in the blades
yet tenacious in the roots
the grass sways in the winds;
it keeps firm to its own ground.
Nailed on its own spot
the grass sobs inwardly.
Tonight as before
it lights a lamp and tends it.
Winds should be made welcome,
for they will make it strong.
All those who are poor,
let not your poverty
bring you low and debased
the way grass never feels
sorry for its grassiness.

MOON, Chung-hee (1947-). A native of Posong, South Cholla province, Moon studied Korean at Tongguk University as an undergraduate and graduate student. She went to New York University for two years as a non-degree student. A series of her first poems came out in **Wolgan Munhak** (Monthly Literature) in 1969. In 1975 she was awarded the Modern Literature Prize. She has to her credit eight volumes of poems: **Flower's Breath** (1969), **Collected Poems** (1973), **Bell-sound Falling on Its Own** (1984), **My Brother's Bird** (1986), **My Sweet Home** (1987), **You're Gone Farther than the Sky** (1988), and **To Young Love** (1991), selected poems.

Poem at Forty

The number seems more honest than the poem.
Turning forty today
skin in the neck firm and bouncy till yesterday at thirty nine
has grown limp and flabby over night,
into a waste mass of cotton wool.

At a funeral strewn
with yellow chrysanthemums
I see myself framed in the place
of the dead m an's photograph
and find myself lamenting over my own death.

I get cross when I have no reason to.
I get scared for no reason whatsoever.
I start forgetting to love
rather than make a cowardly effort
to love again.

What is it to be forty?
All shades of gray on earth
hovering overhead so far
now settles in me into my whole person
and I feel like dialing phone numbers
anywhere to order a new dress made for me

How a mere number crushes my spirit
into a wilted flower on the grass!

A Flock of Birds

Can the river alone run?
Blood runs too into the heaven,
so do dead leaves heavenward,
not knowing where they are from;
each runs as on a gleaming road,
a point of departure.

The last stubborn sleepless hours
painted in dots on the face,
howling in the gleam of light,
O love that lifts upright!
Following in her wake
all of us flow together
and head forever heavenward
without any reason to weep.

KIM, Namju (1946-   ). A native of Haenam, South Cholla province, Kim was admitted to Chonnam National University in 1968 but was soon forced to leave because of his political activism. As a student, he edited an underground newspaper "Outcry" in a move to oppose the dictatorial rule. Since 1973 his life has been spent in on-and-off imprisonment. Again in 1988 he was sentenced to 15 years and was released on parole in 1988 on the strength of petitions by writers at home and International P.E.N. members. His first collected poems **Requiem** came out in 1984, followed by **My Sword and My Blood** (1987), **My Country Is One** (1988), **Love's Weapon** (1989), **Let's Speak Out** (1989) and **The Abode of Ideas** (1992). Kim's work as a whole is strongly tinged with ideological protest against capitalistic exploitation.

This Autumn

This autumn, in blue prisoner's garb, hands tied behind my back,
feet in manacles, I am taken to another part of the country.
Where am I being carried now, I wonder, to Chonju jail or Kwangju
or somewhere else? My jail van runs out of the crowded street
of a familiar city onto the middle of fields. I wish to get off
here from the coop and to head to my mother who is picking
peppers in the field with a hot sun on her back, to join my father who
is harvesting in the paddy-field bending his newly-sharpened sickle,
and to play with the children who form a circle on the bank urging
sheep to horn each other for a fight.
I wish to get off free from ropes and chains. I wish to run
freely with my son, our arms spread out skyward.
I wish to run till my ankles grown numb in the paddy path;
I wish to run with the wind blowing full in my breast;
I wish to run till I grow out of breath.
When thirsty, I'll cup my hands to drink from a roadside spring-well;
when hungry, I will pull out a radish by the roots beside the road
and feed on it along the endless road I take, and when tired at
the close of day I will head homeward the way homing birds do.
But the prison car never stops but continues on its way crossing
field after field. Now it is crossing the historic river on which
farmers rose up a long time ago to fight the corrupt government;
the farmer-militia defeated the nobles and rich as they advanced
on this hilly pass to seize the provincial capital. I am crossing the
same pass, the old battle site. This autumn, in a blue prison uniform...

Spring Comes to the Hills and Fields

Someone asked me in passing:
''Where is he now?''
He's gone *there*, I said.

Where is there? he asked, pointing
to a white-washed building behind the wall.
Where freedom writhes to shake off the bondage.

With the springtime arriving on the hills and fields
someone asked me in passing:
Hasn't he been freed yet?
Pointing to a grave
I said he is there now.

Index of Poets *

* As for the romanization of Korean, the author has adopted the McCune-Reischauer transcription system. Exceptions are made of preferred personal names. *Park* is more preferred than *Pak*. But in place of *Lee* or *Rhee Yi* has been employed.